LEARN FRENCH IN 100 DAYS

THE 100% NATURAL METHOD TO FINALLY GET RESULTS WITH FRENCH!

BEGINNER

NATURA LINGUA

NATURA
LINGUA

LEARN FRENCH IN 100 DAYS

TABLE OF CONTENTS

CONGRATULATIONS AND NEXT STEPS

WELCOME

Imagine: you're walking around in Paris, understanding and speaking French naturally. Phrases spontaneously emerge in your mind, and you navigate this new language with ease and fluidity.

That's the goal of this manual.

If you're reading these lines, it's because you wish to master French. Whether for work or pleasure, the goal remains the same: to achieve it. The problem lies in the lack of time. Good courses to learn French in English are rare, and often, the available methods are complicated or ineffective.

But your motivation is intact! That's why you've tried apps promising wonders in just a few minutes a day. The result? More time spent collecting badges than acquiring real skills in French. You've tried traditional textbooks, often too complex and focused on grammar. Perhaps you've even considered classical courses, incompatible with your schedule.

My name is François, and I'm French. I am well acquainted with this situation.

A few years ago, I went to do a year of volunteering in Ukraine. To be effective, I had to quickly learn Russian and English. But most learning resources were either too superficial or too complex.

Even worse, despite my motivation and long hours in front of my screen or immersed in manuals, the results were not forthcoming. I felt frustrated, angry, wondering why language learning seemed so easy for some and so difficult for me.

I was about to give up, thinking I was not cut out for languages.

Then, one evening, I met an English polyglot who spoke 11 languages. Impressed by his linguistic abilities, I asked him for his secret. His answer, as simple as it was unexpected, was that one should not study a language, but live it! One must learn a new language as one learned their mother tongue.

Intrigued, I followed his advice.

After all, I hadn't learned my mother tongue through conjugation tables or collecting badges. No, I learned French by imitating those around me, by communicating with my friends and family.

So, I abandoned my textbooks and removed the conjugation tables from the walls of my room.

I started listening to podcasts in English, watching movies in Russian, and engaging in my first conversations. Forgetting grammar and conjugation, I simply used these languages. The results were quick to come: I increasingly understood daily conversations, with words and phrases naturally coming to mind.

My English friend was right: it worked.

Just as it's more effective to learn to swim by jumping into the water rather than reading a book on swimming, learning a foreign language is done by immersing oneself in the language, practicing conversation, listening, and adapting to the culture and linguistic nuances, rather than limiting oneself to the theoretical study of grammar rules and vocabulary.

This is the approach I propose in this Natura Lingua manual.

From the first lesson, you will fully immerse yourself in French.

In a few days, or even weeks, you will start to build a lexical foundation and mental mechanisms that will allow you to understand and communicate naturally in most daily situations.

Be aware, Natura Lingua is not a miracle solution. To get results, you will need to follow one lesson a day for 100 days.

But if you're ready to make this effort, then anyone can succeed with our method, based directly on the mechanisms that allowed you to learn your mother tongue.

If you've already learned your mother tongue, why couldn't you learn French?

Courage,

François

THE NATURALINGUA METHOD

Natura Lingua offers you a natural and intuitive approach that transforms the language learning experience. Every educational content is meticulously optimized to enable you to acquire a new language up to 10 times faster and more efficiently than traditional methods.

Each Natura Lingua manual is based on four innovative principles that reinvent the way languages are learned.

1. The Funnel Principle

We've rigorously analyzed and filtered hundreds of thousands of words to retain only those that are essential in daily conversations. Thanks to this principle, you quickly develop a high level of understanding without wasting your time on superfluous terms.

2. Contextual Assimilation

Each term is introduced in a natural setting, reflecting common daily interactions. The result? A smooth assimilation of hundreds of terms and expressions, without ever feeling like you're actually studying.

3. Progressive Overload

Each lesson meticulously presents new words while reintroducing those already studied. Thus, day by day, you continuously progress while consolidating what you've learned.

4. <u>Multiple Integrated Revisions</u>

Gone are the days when vocabulary seemed to evaporate from your memory. Our unique method ensures that each term is reintroduced at strategic intervals in subsequent lessons. You revisit each term up to four times, reinforcing its memorization without even realizing it.

The Mechanism

What makes "Natura Lingua" so effective is its natural and gradual learning. Each lesson introduces new words in bold while reusing words from previous lessons. Additionally, each lesson is enriched with a "Grammatical Note" to illuminate key aspects of the language and a "Cultural Note" to avoid faux pas during conversations with natives.

Is It For Me?

If you're looking to speak a new language without getting lost in the intricacies of grammar, this manual is for you. However, if you love complex grammatical rules and endless vocabulary lists, then this manual is not for you.

Integrating the Manual Into Your Daily Life

Create a routine: dedicate a slot each day for your 15-minute lesson. A coffee in hand, your manual open in front of you, and off you go!

NB. I highly recommend downloading the audio that accompanies the lessons. It will greatly enhance your understanding and pronunciation. Using this manual without the audio is like enjoying toast without jam: you're missing the essence.

ADDITIONAL RESOURCES

DOWNLOAD THE RESOURCES ASSOCIATED
WITH THIS MANUAL AND GREATLY
ENHANCE YOUR CHANCES OF SUCCESS.

Scan this QR code to access them:

☞ **https://www.natura-lingua.com/download**

• **Optimize your learning with audio:** To significantly improve your language skills, we strongly advise you to download the audio files accompanying this manual. This will enhance your listening comprehension and pronunciation.

• **Enhance your learning with flashcards:** Flashcards are excellent tools for vocabulary memorization. We highly encourage you to use them to maximize your results. Download our set of cards, specially designed for this manual.

• **Join our learning community:** If you're looking to connect with other language enthusiasts through "Natura Lingua", we invite you to join our online group. In this community, you'll have the opportunity to ask questions, find learning partners, and share your progress.

• **Explore more with other Natura Lingua manuals:** If you like this method, note that there are other similar manuals for different languages. Discover our complete collection of manuals to enrich your linguistic learning experience in a natural and progressive way.

We are here to support you in learning the target language. For optimal results, we highly recommend downloading the audio and using the flashcards. These additional resources are designed to further facilitate your journey.

Happy learning!

BEFORE BEGINNING

DEBUNKING MYTHS ABOUT
LEARNING FRENCH

French, often referred to as the language of love, has captivated millions of learners worldwide with its melodious sounds and rich cultural heritage. However, the path to mastering French is frequently clouded by misconceptions that can deter potential learners. Let's debunk some of these myths and shed light on the true essence of learning French.

Myth 1: French is an Extremely Difficult Language to Learn

One of the most pervasive myths about learning French is its supposed difficulty. While French does have its complexities, such as gendered nouns and verb conjugations, it's important to remember that difficulty is subjective. English speakers will find many similarities in vocabulary due to the significant influence of French on the English language. The Common European Framework of Reference for Languages (CEFR) even classifies French as a Category 1 language for

English speakers, indicating it is among the easier languages to learn.

Myth 2: You Need to Move to a French-Speaking Country to Become Fluent

While immersion is undoubtedly beneficial, the digital age has brought the world closer. Online platforms, language exchange apps, and virtual reality environments offer immersive experiences from the comfort of your home. Success stories abound of individuals achieving fluency through online courses, dedicated practice, and engagement with French media.

Myth 3: You're Too Old to Learn French

Another myth is the belief that language learning is only for the young. Research in neuroplasticity has shown that adult brains are more than capable of acquiring new languages. The key is consistent practice and a positive mindset. Adults often have the advantage of better metacognitive skills and can apply learning strategies more effectively than younger learners.

Myth 4: You Must Have a "Language Gene" to Learn French

The idea that you need to be born with a special talent to learn languages is a myth that undermines the efforts of language learners. Success in language learning comes down to motivation, effective study habits, and exposure. Stories of polyglots who learned multiple languages later in life, often without any perceived innate talent, serve as inspiration for learners at any stage.

Myth 5: It Takes Years to Make Any Real Progress

This myth can be particularly demotivating. Progress in language learning is not linear and depends on various factors, including the learner's goals, consistency, and the methods used. Many learners achieve conversational fluency within months by focusing on practical language use, engaging with native speakers, and immersing themselves in French media.

The Real Challenge: Overcoming the Plateau

While debunking these myths offers a more encouraging perspective on learning French, it's essential to acknowledge the real challenge: the intermediate plateau. Many learners find that after initial rapid progress, their advancement slows. The key to overcoming this plateau is diversification of learning strategies, seeking out challenging material, and maintaining a routine that includes speaking, listening, reading, and writing.

Learning French, like any language, is a journey with its ups and downs. The myths surrounding its difficulty can deter learners before they even begin. However, by understanding that these preconceived ideas are more fiction than fact, potential learners can approach the language with a renewed sense of possibility. The real challenge isn't in starting but in pushing through the intermediate plateau with perseverance and a love for the language. With the right mindset and strategies, anyone can learn French and open the door to a rich world of cultural and personal growth.

THE POLYGLOTS' SECRET

Have you ever thought that learning multiple languages was only for geniuses? Take Cardinal Giuseppe Mezzofanti, for example—he's said to have spoken between 38 and 72 languages, depending on the source. And what makes it even more impressive is that he did it in a time without the internet, apps, or all the resources we have today. Another amazing example is Kato Lomb, a Hungarian interpreter who spoke 16 languages fluently and could handle 11 more.

But how did they do it?

These language masters understood something many people miss. Learning a language doesn't have to mean complicated textbooks, intense courses, or years of effort. Mezzofanti and Lomb used a simpler, more natural approach. For them, learning wasn't a chore or an impossible task—it was a smooth, almost instinctive process.

. . .

What if learning a language wasn't as hard as you think?

A lot of people believe that becoming a polyglot takes a special gift or years of hard work. But that's not true. Learning a language is often much easier than it seems. What feels like a huge challenge is really just about using the right method.

Mezzofanti learned by translating religious texts, while Kato Lomb translated foreign books she found in libraries. This helped them learn quickly and naturally. Their secret? Consistency and immersion through translation. By translating texts from a foreign language into their own, and then back again, they slowly mastered the language.

So how can you do the same?

You don't need expensive courses or complicated techniques. Start with simple texts in the language you want to learn, translate them into your own language, and then back again. This simple method helps you absorb the language and its structure naturally.

Now's the time to get started.

With the NaturaLingua method, inspired by the natural approaches of Mezzofanti and Lomb, you can finally break through the language barrier. Don't let fear or misconceptions stop you. Jump in and enjoy the process of learning, understanding, and speaking a new language, one translation at a time. Are you ready to take on the challenge and add new languages to your life?

WHY LEARNING FRENCH ?

If you're reading this text, it's because you're interested in learning French. That's a fantastic choice! French is not just a language; it's a key to unlocking a rich tapestry of culture, history, and art. But before we dive into the beauty of French, let's talk about motivation. It's the fuel that keeps the engine of learning running, even when the road gets tough.

1. Unlock the World of French Culture: Imagine being able to read the works of Victor Hugo, Marcel Proust, or Simone de Beauvoir in their original language. French literature offers a window into the soul of its people and an insight into human nature itself.

2. Enhance Your Travel Experiences: France is the world's top tourist destination, and speaking French opens up a whole new dimension of travel experiences. From ordering in a Parisian café to conversing with locals in the picturesque villages of Provence, French allows you to connect on a deeper level.

3. Boost Your Career Opportunities: French is an official language in over 29 countries and is a significant language in international relations, business, and the arts. Learning French can open doors to international job opportunities and elevate your professional profile.

4. Connect with a Global Community: French is spoken by over 275 million people worldwide. Learning French enables you to connect with a vast network of people, fostering personal and professional relationships across continents.

5. Challenge Yourself: Learning a new language is a fantastic way to stimulate your brain, improve cognitive skills, and even delay the onset of dementia. French, with its rich vocabulary and clear structure, is an excellent choice for those looking to challenge themselves.

6. Access to Higher Education: French universities are among the top in the world, and many programs offer courses in English and French. Proficiency in French can open up opportunities for scholarships and studies in France and other Francophone countries.

. . .

7. It's Beautiful and Fun: French is often called the language of love for its melodious sound and expressive nuances. Learning French is not just about grammar and vocabulary; it's about embracing the joy and romance of the Francophone world.

In conclusion, learning French is a journey that offers far more than the ability to communicate. It's a passport to a richer, more fulfilling life. So, let this be your call to action: embrace the challenge, persevere through the difficulties, and never give up on your dream of speaking French. The rewards, both tangible and intangible, are limitless. Bon voyage on your journey to learning French!

INSTRUCTIONS

SIMPLE FRENCH
PRONUNCIATION

Welcome to your quick guide to French pronunciation! This guide will help you get started with the basics. Remember, practice makes perfect, so keep trying and listening to native speakers whenever possible.

Vowels

- **A** like in "father" (e.g., "papa" [pah-pah])
- **E** has several sounds:

  - Like "uh" in "sofa" when it's at the end of a word (e.g., "le" [luh])
  - Like "ay" in "say" when accented (é) (e.g., "été" [ay-tay])
  - More closed, like "e" in "bed" without the final d sound, especially in "er" endings (e.g., "manger" [mahn-zhay])

- **I** like "ee" in "see" (e.g., "si" [see])

- **O** can be like "o" in "so" (e.g., "eau" [oh]) or like "aw" in "saw" without the w sound (e.g., "porte" [port])
- **U** is a unique sound not found in English. Round your lips as if to say "oo" in "food," but try to say "ee" (e.g., "lune" [loon])
- **Y** in French is treated like "i" (e.g., "style" [steel])

Consonants

- **R** is guttural, pronounced in the back of the throat (e.g., "rouge" [roozh]). Think of a soft gargle.
- **T** is softer than in English, more like "t" in "stall" (e.g., "tarte" [tart])
- **S** is usually a clear "s" sound as in "snake" unless it's between vowels, then it sounds like "z" (e.g., "poison" [pwah-zohn])
- **H** is always silent (e.g., "heure" [ur])
- **J** like "s" in "measure" (e.g., "je" [zhuh])
- **G** before e or i sounds like "s" in "measure" (e.g., "girafe" [zhee-raf])

Nasal Sounds

Nasal sounds are unique to French and occur when "n" or "m" follows a vowel in the same syllable. Do not pronounce the "n" or "m" but instead let the air flow through your nose.

- **AN/AM** like "ah" in "father" but nasal (e.g., "an" [ahn])
- **EN/EM** same as "AN/AM" (e.g., "enfant" [ahn-fahn])
- **IN/IM** like "ang" in "bang" without the g sound, but nasal (e.g., "vin" [van])
- **ON/OM** like "own" but nasal (e.g., "nom" [nohm])
- **UN/UM** is a bit like "ung" in "hung" without the g sound, but nasal and with a tighter mouth shape (e.g., "parfum" [par-fun])

Final Tips

- **Liaisons** are important in French. They occur when a normally silent consonant at the end of a word is pronounced because the next word begins with a vowel or silent h (e.g., "les amis" [lay-zah-mee]).
- **Accent marks** can change the pronunciation of vowels, especially "é" (ay) and "è" (eh).
- **Silent letters** are common at the end of words, especially "s," "t," and "d."

Practice these sounds, and don't be afraid to exaggerate them as you learn. Listening to French speakers and repeating after them is one of the best ways to improve your pronunciation. Bonne chance (Good luck)!

HOW TO USE THIS MANUAL

Phase No. 1:

1. Read the text in the language you are learning out loud, while listening to the corresponding audio (to be downloaded).
2. Try to translate the text into English, without consulting the translation.
3. Check with the official translation to complete yours.

This phase facilitates the assimilation of the language structure and vocabulary and reinforces understanding.

ДЕНЬ 1: ПРИВІТАННЯ

1. Привіт, як справи?
2. Добре, дякую. А у вас?
3. Теж добре, дякую. Доброго ранку!
4. Доброго ранку! Чи можу я вам допомогти?
5. Будь ласка, де тут банк?
6. Прямо за рогом. До зустрічі!
7. Дякую! До побачення!
8. Доброго дня!
9. Добрий вечір! Добраніч!

❖ In Ukraine, it's traditional to greet those close friends with three kisses on the cheeks or neither.

Handwritten annotations:

Hello, how are you doing?
Doing well, thank you. And you?
Also doing well, thank you. Good morning.
Good morning! Can I assist you with something?
Yes, please. Where is the bank located?
It's just around the corner. See you later!
Thank you! Goodbye!
Have a good day!
Good evening! Good night!

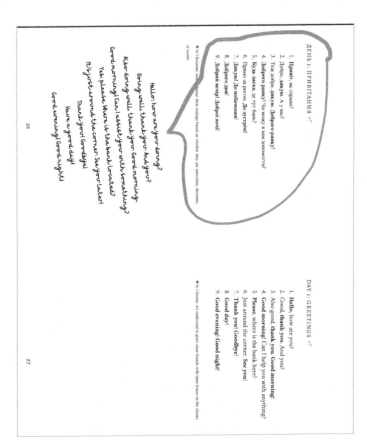

DAY 1: GREETINGS

1. **Hello, how are you?**
2. Good, **thank you. And you?**
3. Also good, **thank you. Good morning!**
4. **Good morning!** Can I help you with anything?
5. **Please,** where is the bank here?
6. Just around the corner. **See you!**
7. **Thank you! Goodbye!**
8. **Good day!**
9. **Good evening! Good night!**

❖ In Ukraine, it's traditional to greet close friends with three kisses on the cheeks or neither.

Phase No. 1

Phase No. 2 (starting from lesson No. 7):

1. For each lesson starting from No. 7, first translate the text of that lesson (No. 7, No. 8, etc.) from the target language into English.
2. Then, go back 6 lessons and translate the English version of that lesson's text from English back into the target language, without referring to the original text.
3. Compare your translation with the original text of that lesson and adjust if necessary.
4. Read aloud the original text of that lesson, while listening to the audio.

This phase stimulates the activation of already acquired vocabulary and promotes the improvement of your communication skills.

ДЕНЬ 1: ПРИВІТАННЯ ✓

1. **Привіт**, як справи?
2. Добре, дякую. А у вас?
3. Теж добре, дякую. Доброго ранку!
4. **Доброго ранку!** Чи можу я вам допомогти?
5. **Будь ласка**, де тут банк?
6. Прямо за рогом. До зустрічі!
7. **Дякую!** До побачення!
8. Доброго дня!
9. Добрий вечір! Доброї ночі!

❖ In Ukrainian, nouns change their endings based on whether they are masculine, feminine, or neuter.

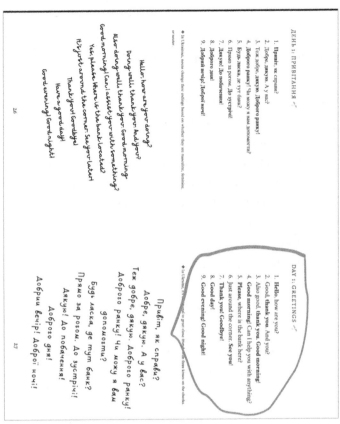

Hello, how are you doing?

Being well, thank you. And you?

Also doing well, thank you. Good morning!

Good morning! Can I assist you with something?

Yes, please. Where is the bank located?

It's just around the corner. See you later!

Thank you! Goodbye!

Have a good day!

Good evening! Good night!

DAY 1: GREETINGS ✓

1. **Hello**, how are you?
2. Good, thank you. And you?
3. Also good, thank you. Good morning!
4. **Good morning!** Can I help you with anything!
5. **Please**, where is the bank here?
6. Just around the corner. See you!
7. **Thank you!** Goodbye!
8. **Good day!**
9. Good evening! Good night!

❖ In Ukraine, it's usual to greet people with three kisses on the cheeks.

Привіт, як справи?

Добре, дякую. А у вас?

Теж добре, дякую. Доброго ранку!

Доброго ранку! Чи можу я вам допомогти?

Будь ласка, де тут банк?

Прямо за рогом. До зустрічі!

Дякую! До побачення!

Доброго дня!

Добрий вечір! Доброї ночі!

Phase No. 2

Continue in the same way for the following lessons. For example, for lesson No. 8, first translate the text of lesson No. 8 from the target language into English, then translate the text of lesson No. 2 from English back into the target language, and so on.

Additionally, every 10 lessons, a small challenge awaits you to put your knowledge into practice.

Note: Your translations do not need to match the manual texts perfectly, but they should convey a similar meaning. If you are using the paper version of the manual, note your translations directly at the bottom of the text, or else use a separate notebook.

AND WHAT ABOUT GRAMMAR?

You've probably been told that mastering a language starts with grammar. But this traditional approach is not only discouraging, it's also counterproductive. Learning a language is really about diving into a living world and understanding how words and sentences come to life in real situations, not by endlessly reciting rules.

One of the biggest mistakes many learners make is trying to memorize grammar rules by heart. It's tedious, demotivating, and ineffective. Why? Because our brains remember things that make sense and are used regularly. Rules without context are quickly forgotten. It's disconnected from real-life learning: instead of speaking, feeling, and immersing yourself in the language, you end up drowning in sterile theories.

We strongly believe that grammar shouldn't be learned before using a language, but rather through natural usage.

Our method is based on a simple principle: start by using the language, then adjust your understanding of grammar as it comes up in real-life situations. You learn to speak and understand, just like a child discovering their native language. When a grammar question arises, you find the answer and remember it because it's relevant at that moment.

How does it work in practice?

1. Immerse yourself in the language without worrying about grammar rules at first.
2. When a grammar question naturally comes up ("Why is this word used here?"), look for the answer.
3. Write down the grammar points you come across on a separate page or in the blank section of this manual, like a grammar journal.
4. Keep repeating this process, question after question, and watch how your understanding grows without feeling like you're studying.

By using this method, you'll see real results: each grammar point is anchored in a real context, making it easier to remember and longer-lasting. Instead of getting stuck in grammar books, you'll be using the language right away, gaining confidence and fluency in your communication. Plus, you'll enjoy it more—learning becomes an exciting journey where each discovery is a personal victory.

Grammar will become an ally, not a hurdle, helping you progress naturally and smoothly.

With Natura Lingua, you're not following a rigid method— you're living the language. Grammar is no longer a mountain to climb, but a natural path that unfolds as you go, step by step.

ADDITIONAL RESOURCES

DOWNLOAD THE RESOURCES ASSOCIATED WITH THIS MANUAL AND GREATLY ENHANCE YOUR CHANCES OF SUCCESS.

Scan this QR code to access them:

👉 **https://www.natura-lingua.com/download**

• **Optimize your learning with audio:** To significantly improve your language skills, we strongly advise you to download the audio files accompanying this manual. This will enhance your listening comprehension and pronunciation.

- **Enhance your learning with flashcards:** Flashcards are excellent tools for vocabulary memorization. We highly encourage you to use them to maximize your results. Download our set of cards, specially designed for this manual.

- **Join our learning community:** If you're looking to connect with other language enthusiasts through "Natura Lingua", we invite you to join our online group. In this community, you'll have the opportunity to ask questions, find learning partners, and share your progress.

- **Explore more with other Natura Lingua manuals:** If you like this method, note that there are other similar manuals for different languages. Discover our complete collection of manuals to enrich your linguistic learning experience in a natural and progressive way.

We are here to support you in learning the target language. For optimal results, we highly recommend downloading the audio and using the flashcards. These additional resources are designed to further facilitate your journey.

Happy learning!

FRENCH IN 100 DAYS

Check off a box below after completing each lesson. This will aid you in monitoring your progress and maintaining motivation throughout your learning experience.

IMPORTANT NOTES :

1. **The Essentials: Vocabulary and Key Phrases:** In each Natura Lingua lesson, we carefully select the most useful words and expressions relevant to the theme studied. The goal is to familiarize you with the most frequently used constructions in the target language. Sometimes, the general meaning of the texts might seem surprising, but don't worry, it's an essential part of our method. It helps you focus on the practical aspects of the language, thereby accelerating your learning for better understanding and more effective communication.

2. **Translation: As Close to the Original as Possible:** We translate in a way that stays true to the source text, capturing how sentences are structured and ideas are conveyed in the target language. Our goal is not syntactic perfection in English, but rather to give you an authentic insight into the thought process and structure of the language you are learning. This method immerses you in the language, allowing you to gain a more natural and intuitive understanding. Our aim is to help you think and communicate fluently in the learned language, not just understand it. We want to prepare you to use the language practically and confidently in your daily life.

1. **Bonjour**, comment ça va ?
2. Ça va bien, **merci**. Et toi ?
3. Très bien, **merci**. **Au revoir** et **bonne après-midi**.
4. **Salut ! À plus tard**.
5. **Bonsoir**. Comment s'est passée ta journée ?
6. Bien, **merci**. **Bonne nuit**.
7. **De rien. Au revoir**.

✣ In French, nouns that refer to people or animals often have a masculine or feminine form, like "ami" (friend) for a male and "amie" for a female.

DAY 1: GREETINGS

1. **Hello**, how are you?
2. I'm good, **thank you**. And you?
3. Very well, **thank you**. **Goodbye** and **have a good afternoon**.
4. **Hi! See you later**.
5. **Good evening**. How was your day?
6. Good, **thank you**. **Good night**.
7. **You're welcome. Goodbye**.

✤ In France, it's common to greet friends with a cheek kiss, the number of which varies by region.

1. **Bonjour**, comment ça va ?
2. **Salut** ! Ça va bien, **et** toi ?
3. Pas mal. Tu veux aller au cinéma ce soir ?
4. **Peut-être**. Quel film ?
5. Un **petit** film indépendant.
6. **D'accord. Excuse-moi**, c'est à quelle heure ?
7. À 8 heures.
8. **Désolé**, je ne peux pas. J'ai un autre engagement.
9. **Au revoir** alors, **merci** quand même.

✤ In French, verbs change their endings to match the subject of the sentence.

DAY 2: COMMON EXPRESSIONS 🌱

1. **Hello**, how are you?
2. **Hi**! I'm good, **and** you?
3. Not bad. Do you want to go to the movies tonight?
4. **Maybe**. Which movie?
5. A **small** independent film.
6. **Okay**. **Excuse me**, what time is it at?
7. At 8 o'clock.
8. **Sorry**, I can't. I have another commitment.
9. **Goodbye** then, **thank you** anyway.

♣ The French expression "l'appel du vide," literally meaning "the call of the void," describes the inexplicable urge to jump when in a high place.

1. **Bonjour ! Je suis un homme. Et vous ?**
2. **Bonjour ! Je suis une femme. Comment allez-vous ?**
3. **Je vais bien, merci ! Et vous, comment allez-vous ?**
4. **Je vais bien aussi, merci. Comment vous appelez-vous ?**
5. **Je m'appelle Marc. Et vous, comment vous appelez-vous ?**
6. **Je m'appelle Sophie. Quel âge avez-vous ?**
7. **J'ai 25 ans. Et vous, quel âge avez-vous ?**
8. **J'ai 30 ans.**
9. **D'accord. Excusez-moi, je dois y aller. Au revoir !**

✤ In French, adjectives usually come after the noun they describe, unlike in English.

DAY 3: INTRODUCTION VOCABULARY

1. Hello! I am a man. And you?
2. Hello! I am a woman. How are you?
3. I'm fine, thank you! And you, how are you?
4. I'm fine too, thank you. What's your name?
5. My name is Marc. And you, what's your name?
6. My name is Sophie. How old are you?
7. I am 25 years old. And you, how old are you?
8. I am 30 years old.
9. Okay. Excuse me, I have to go. Goodbye!

✤ In France, it's customary to greet each person individually with a handshake or cheek kisses, even in a group setting, to show respect and acknowledgment.

1. Salut ! **D'où viens-tu ?**
2. **Je viens de Paris.** Et toi ?
3. **J'habite à Lyon. Que fais-tu dans la vie ?**
4. **Je suis enseignant. Qu'est-ce que tu aimes ?**
5. **J'aime la musique et le sport.** Et toi, quel est ton âge ?
6. J'ai 25 ans. **Enchanté de te rencontrer !**
7. **Enchanté aussi. Bonne journée !**
8. **Merci, au revoir !**
9. **Bonsoir !**

✤ In French, use "le" for masculine nouns, "la" for feminine nouns, and "les" for plural nouns when talking about specific things, like "le nom" (the name), "la ville" (the city), and "les adresses" (the addresses).

1. Hello! **Where are you from?**
2. **I'm from Paris.** And you?
3. **I live in Lyon. What do you do for a living?**
4. **I'm a teacher. What do you like?**
5. **I like music and sports.** And you, how old are you?
6. I'm 25 years old. **Nice to meet you!**
7. **Nice to meet you too. Have a good day!**
8. **Thank you, goodbye!**
9. **Good evening!**

✤ In France, it's common to exchange cheek kisses upon meeting, but sharing one's phone number can take much longer to achieve.

1. **Excusez-moi, je comprends un peu le français. Je viens** de commencer à apprendre.
2. **Je sais. Je peux t'aider si tu veux.**
3. **J'ai besoin** de pratiquer. **Je fais** des erreurs.
4. **Je vais** t'enseigner. **Tu habites** ici maintenant ?
5. Oui, **j'habite** ici. **J'ai** un appartement.
6. **Je regarde** souvent des films pour apprendre. **Tu aimes** les films français ?
7. Oui, **j'aime** beaucoup. **Je voudrais acheter** des livres aussi.
8. **Je donne** des cours de français. **Tu peux** venir si **tu veux.**
9. **D'accord, je vais y réfléchir. Merci**, enchanté.

✤ In French, use "un" for masculine nouns and "une" for feminine nouns before a verb to mean "a" or "an."

1. **Excuse me, I understand** a little French. **I just** started learning.
2. **I know**. **I can help you if you want**.
3. **I need** to practice. **I make** mistakes.
4. **I will** teach you. **Do you live** here now?
5. Yes, **I live** here. **I have** an apartment.
6. **I often watch** movies to learn. **Do you like** French movies?
7. Yes, **I really like** them. **I would like** to **buy** books too.
8. **I give** French lessons. **You can** come if **you want**.
9. **Alright, I will think about it. Thank you**, nice to meet you.

✣ In French, the verb "tutoyer" means to address someone informally, highlighting the culture's nuanced approach to respect and familiarity.

1. Bonjour, je voudrais **boire** un **thé**, s'il vous plaît.

2. Bien sûr, et pour moi, je vais prendre un **café**. Merci.

3. Vous avez quel **âge** ? Parce que je peux aussi recommander une bonne **bière**.

4. J'ai vingt-deux ans, mais aujourd'hui, je préfère quelque chose sans alcool. Peut-être de l'**eau** ou un **soda**.

5. D'accord, et pour moi, un **jus** d'orange et un verre de **vin** rouge, s'il vous plaît.

6. Je comprends. Vous voulez quelque chose à manger avec vos **boissons** ?

7. Non, merci. Juste les **boissons** pour l'instant.

8. Et pour l'enfant, un **lait** chaud, s'il vous plaît.

9. Bien sûr, je vous apporte ça tout de suite. Merci beaucoup.

✤ In French, when talking about liking beverages, use the pronoun "en" to replace phrases introduced by "de" such as "J'en bois" meaning "I drink some."

1. Hello, I would like to **drink** a **tea**, please.
2. Of course, and for me, I'll have a **coffee**. Thank you.
3. How **old** are you? Because I can also recommend a good **beer**.
4. I'm twenty-two years old, but today, I'd prefer something non-alcoholic. Maybe some **water** or a **soda**.
5. Alright, and for me, an **orange juice** and a glass of **red wine**, please.
6. I understand. Would you like anything to eat with your **drinks**?
7. No, thank you. Just the **drinks** for now.
8. And for the child, a warm **milk**, please.
9. Sure, I'll bring that right over. Thank you very much.

✤ In France, sharing a bottle of Champagne is a symbol of celebration and luxury, originating from its royal associations and the region's strict production laws.

Important Reminder Before Starting Lesson 7

* * *

Congratulations on your progress so far! You are about to embark on a crucial stage of your learning: Phase No. 2.

Please follow these instructions starting from lesson 7:

- For each lesson from No. 7 onward, first translate the text of that lesson (No. 7, No. 8, etc.) from the target language into English.
- Then, go back 6 lessons and translate the English version of that lesson's text from English back into the target language, without referring to the original text.
- Compare your translation with the original text of that lesson and adjust if necessary.
- Read the original text of that lesson out loud, while listening to the audio.

This new phase is designed to activate the vocabulary you have already assimilated. Keep up the momentum and enjoy this enriching new phase of your learning!

JOUR 7 : ADJECTIFS DESCRIPTIFS I ✎

1. Bonjour, tu **viens** d'où ?
2. Je **viens** de Paris. Et toi, d'où **viens**-tu ?
3. Je **viens** de Lyon. Qu'est-ce que tu **fais** ici ?
4. Je suis ici pour le travail. Et toi, qu'est-ce que tu **aimes** boire ?
5. J'**aime** le **thé chaud et le café fort**. Et toi ?
6. Moi, j'**aime** l'**eau froide** et la **bière froide**. Tu **habites** où à Paris ?
7. J'**habite** dans un **petit** appartement **nouveau**. Et toi, à Lyon ?
8. Dans une **grande** maison, mais elle est **vieille**. **Enchanté** de te rencontrer.
9. **Enchanté** aussi.

✤ In French, adjectives usually come after the noun they describe, but adverbs describing how something is done come before the verb.

DAY 7: DESCRIPTIVE ADJECTIVES I 🌱

1. Hello, where are you **from**?
2. I'm **from** Paris. And you, where are you **from**?
3. I'm **from** Lyon. What are you **doing** here?
4. I'm here for work. And you, what do you **like** to drink?
5. I **like hot tea** and **strong coffee**. And you?
6. I **like cold water** and **cold beer**. Where do you **live** in Paris?
7. I **live** in a **small new** apartment. And you, in Lyon?
8. In a **big** house, but it's **old**. Nice to meet you.
9. Nice to meet you too.

✤ French novels often use "lumineuse" (luminous) to describe Paris, reflecting the city's nickname, "The City of Light."

1. Excusez-moi, je voudrais aller à la bibliothèque. C'est **loin** d'**ici** ?
2. Non, c'est **près**. Allez **tout droit**, puis tournez à **droite**.
3. **Par ici ou par là** après **droite** ?
4. **Par là**, après le café. La bibliothèque est **dans** le grand bâtiment **à gauche**.
5. **Là-bas**, près du parc ?
6. Oui, exactement. Vous ne pouvez pas vous tromper, c'est très **facile**.
7. Je comprends. Merci beaucoup !
8. De rien. Bonne journée !

✤ In French, to say "at" or "to" a place, use "à" before the name of the location.

1. Excuse me, I would like to go to the library. Is it **far** from **here**?
2. No, it's **close**. Go **straight ahead**, then turn **right**.
3. **This way or that way** after turning **right**?
4. **That way**, past the café. The library is **in** the big building **on the left**.
5. **Over there**, near the park?
6. Yes, exactly. You can't miss it, it's very **easy**.
7. I understand. Thank you very much!
8. You're welcome. Have a good day!

✤ The Eiffel Tower was originally intended to be dismantled after 20 years but was saved because it proved valuable for communication purposes.

1. Excusez-moi, où est le café **au-dessus** de la librairie ?
2. **À côté** du cinéma, **tournez à gauche** puis **à droite.**
3. Et pour aller **au sud, derrière** le musée ?
4. **Tournez à droite** et continuez **tout droit. Arrêtez-vous ici pour du thé** ou continuez **là-bas** pour de la **bière.**
5. Merci ! Et si je veux de l'**eau** ou un **soda** ?
6. **Sous le pont, il y a un petit magasin à gauche.**
7. Parfait, merci beaucoup !

✤ In French, to give directions, we often use the conjunction "et" (and) to connect two instructions, like "Tournez à gauche et continuez tout droit" (Turn left and continue straight ahead).

1. Excuse me, where is the café **above** the bookstore?
2. **Next to** the cinema, **turn left** then **right**.
3. And to go **south**, **behind** the museum?
4. **Turn right** and continue **straight ahead. Stop here for some tea** or continue **over there for some beer**.
5. Thank you! And if I want some **water** or a **soda**?
6. **Under** the bridge, there's a small store **on the left**.
7. Perfect, thank you so much!

✤ The Eiffel Tower was initially criticized by some of France's leading artists and intellectuals for its design.

1. **Qui** va au marché aujourd'hui ?
2. Moi, **pourquoi** ?
3. **Quoi** vas-tu acheter ?
4. Des fruits. **Lequel** préfères-tu, les pommes ou les oranges ?
5. Les pommes, s'il te plaît. **Où** les trouves-tu ?
6. **Sous** le grand arbre, **à côté** de la boulangerie. **Quand** y vas-tu ?
7. Dans une heure. **Comment** est le temps ?
8. Il fait **chaud** et **beau**. **Ça coûte combien**, les pommes ?
9. Pas cher, mais **combien** en veux-tu ?
10. Trois, s'il te plaît. **Quelle heure est-il** maintenant ?
11. Midi. Je dois y aller **rapidement**.

✤ To form a question with an interjection, start with the interjection followed by a comma, then add your question.

1. **Who** is going to the market today?
2. Me, **why**?
3. **What** are you going to buy?
4. Some fruits. **Which** do you prefer, apples or oranges?
5. Apples, please. **Where** do you find them?
6. **Under** the big tree, **next to** the bakery. **When** are you going?
7. In an hour. **How** is the weather?
8. It's **warm** and **nice**. **How much** are the apples?
9. Not expensive, but **how many** do you want?
10. Three, please. **What time is it** now?
11. Noon. I need to go **quickly**.

✤ In France, the art of conversation is so revered that asking insightful questions is considered a form of flattery.

CHALLENGE NO. 1

CHOOSE A THEME AND CREATE A COLLAGE
OF PHOTOS OR IMAGES, NOTING THE
CORRESPONDING WORD IN FRENCH.

"Petit à petit, l'oiseau fait son nid."

"Little by little, the bird makes its nest."

1. **Aujourd'hui**, il fait beau, n'est-ce pas ?
2. Oui, et **hier**, il pleuvait **toute la journée**.
3. **Demain**, je vais à la plage. Et toi ?
4. Je travaille **demain**, mais **après-demain**, je suis libre.
5. **Maintenant**, je veux manger. Il est quelle **heure** ?
6. Il est midi. Dans une **minute**, nous allons manger.
7. **Hier**, à cette **heure**, j'étais encore au lit.
8. Moi aussi. Le **temps** passe trop vite.
9. Oui, chaque **seconde** est importante.

✤ In French, days of the week are not capitalized unless they start a sentence.

1. **Today**, the weather is nice, isn't it?
2. Yes, and **yesterday**, it was raining **all day**.
3. **Tomorrow**, I'm going to the beach. What about you?
4. I'm working **tomorrow**, but **the day after tomorrow**, I'm free.
5. **Now**, I want to eat. What **time** is it?
6. It's noon. In **one minute**, we're going to eat.
7. **Yesterday**, at this **time**, I was still in bed.
8. Me too. **Time** flies too quickly.
9. Yes, every **second** is important.

✤ In France, discussing the details of one's vacation is a cherished ritual, reflecting the cultural significance of leisure time.

1. **Excusez-moi, quel jour sommes-nous aujourd'hui** ?
2. **Aujourd'hui**, c'est **jeudi**.
3. Et **demain** ?
4. **Demain, c'est vendredi. Après-demain, c'est samedi**.
5. **D'accord**. Et **hier**, c'était **quel jour** ?
6. **Hier, c'était mercredi**.
7. **Peut-être** que je peux faire quelque chose de spécial ce **week-end**.
8. **Oui, samedi et dimanche**, c'est le **week-end**. C'est parfait pour se reposer.
9. **Merci**. Maintenant, je comprends mieux la **semaine**.

✤ In French, days of the week like "lundi" (Monday) don't need an article when talking about recurring events, but you use "le" before the day to mean "on" in specific cases, as in "Le lundi, je fais du sport" (On Mondays, I do sports).

1. **Excuse me, what day is it today?**
2. **Today, it's Thursday.**
3. And **tomorrow?**
4. **Tomorrow, it's Friday. The day after tomorrow, it's Saturday.**
5. **Okay.** And **yesterday**, what day was it?
6. **Yesterday**, it was **Wednesday**.
7. **Maybe I can do something special this weekend.**
8. **Yes, Saturday** and **Sunday**, that's the **weekend.** It's perfect for resting.
9. **Thank you.** Now, I understand the **week** better.

❖ In French, the days of the week are named after Roman gods and celestial bodies, except for Sunday and Monday, which are named after the sun and moon.

1. **Bonjour**! Comment va ta **famille**?
2. Très bien, **merci**. Et la tienne?
3. Bien aussi. Ma **mère** et mon **père** sont chez mes **grands-parents** aujourd'hui.
4. Oh, c'est sympa. Et ton **frère** et ta **sœur**, ils sont avec tes **parents**?
5. Non, mon **frère** est à l'université et ma **sœur** travaille. Et toi, tu as des **enfants**?
6. Pas encore, mais mon **mari** et moi y pensons. Et toi, tu es **marié**?
7. Oui, mon **épouse** et moi avons un fils. Il a cinq ans.
8. Cinq ans! Quel **âge**! **Comment** s'appelle-t-il?
9. Il s'appelle Lucas. Et toi, **pourquoi** pas d'**enfants**?
10. Nous attendons le bon moment. Peut-être l'année prochaine.

✤ In French, to find the direct object in a sentence about family, ask "who?" or "what?" after the verb, like in "J'aime mes parents" (I love my parents), where "mes parents" is the direct object.

1. **Hello!** How is your **family**?
2. Very well, **thank you**. And yours?
3. Good too. My **mother** and **father** are at my **grandparents'** today.
4. Oh, that's nice. And your **brother** and **sister**, are they with your **parents**?
5. No, my **brother** is at university and my **sister** is working. And you, do you have any **children**?
6. Not yet, but my **husband** and I are thinking about it. And you, are you **married**?
7. Yes, my **wife** and I have a son. He is five years old.
8. Five years old! What an **age**! **What** is his name?
9. His name is Lucas. And you, **why** no **children**?
10. We're waiting for the right moment. Maybe next year.

✤ In traditional French families, Sunday lunches can last for hours, symbolizing the importance of family bonding over meals.

1. Bonjour, je suis ton **cousin**. Comment **vas**-tu aujourd'hui?

2. Salut! Je **vais** bien, merci. Et toi, comment **vas**-tu?

3. Très bien, merci. **Hier**, j'ai visité notre **tante** et **oncle**. Ils demandent de tes nouvelles.

4. Ah, c'est gentil! **Maintenant**, je **vis** avec mon **frère** et ma **sœur**.

5. Oh, c'est super! Tu **aimes** vivre avec eux?

6. Oui, beaucoup. Et toi, tu **viens** souvent voir la **famille**?

7. Pas très souvent. Mais **demain**, je vais voir mon **neveu** et ma **nièce**.

8. C'est adorable. Moi, **après-demain**, je vais rencontrer des **amis**.

9. Très bien. **Enchanté** de parler avec toi.

✤ In French, to say you are talking to a family member, use "à" plus a pronoun, like "Je parle à ma sœur" (I am talking to my sister), where "à ma sœur" is the indirect object.

1. Hello, I am your **cousin**. How are you **doing** today?
2. Hi! I'm **doing** well, thank you. And you, how are you **doing**?
3. Very well, thank you. **Yesterday**, I visited our **aunt** and **uncle**. They asked about you.
4. Ah, that's nice! **Now**, I **live** with my **brother** and my **sister**.
5. Oh, that's great! Do you **like** living with them?
6. Yes, a lot. And you, do you often come to see the **family**?
7. Not very often. But **tomorrow**, I'm going to see my **nephew** and my **niece**.
8. That's adorable. Me, **the day after tomorrow**, I'm going to meet some **friends**.
9. Very good. **Nice** talking with you.

✤ In France, the Fête des Lumières in Lyon originally began as a tribute to the Virgin Mary, with families placing candles in their windows to participate in the celebration.

1. Bonjour, je voudrais inviter **trois** cousins, **deux** tantes, et **un** oncle à dîner lundi.

2. D'accord, et combien de neveux et nièces viennent ?

3. **Quatre** neveux et **deux** nièces. Donc, en tout, nous serons **douze**.

4. Je comprends. As-tu besoin d'aide pour préparer ?

5. Oui, je vais faire les courses mercredi et j'ai besoin d'aide pour cuisiner jeudi.

6. Je peux venir jeudi à **cinq** heures. Est-ce que ça va ?

7. Parfait ! Merci beaucoup.

✤ In French, when talking about age with numbers from 1 to 10 in the present tense, use "avoir" (to have) like "J'ai huit ans" (I am 8 years old).

DAY 15: NUMBERS FROM 1 TO 10

1. Hello, I would like to invite **three** cousins, **two** aunts, and **one** uncle to dinner on Monday.
2. Okay, and how many nephews and nieces are coming?
3. **Four** nephews and **two** nieces. So, in total, we will be **twelve**.
4. I understand. Do you need help with the preparation?
5. Yes, I'm going shopping on Wednesday and I need help with cooking on Thursday.
6. I can come on Thursday at **five** o'clock. Does that work?
7. Perfect! Thank you so much.

✣ In France, the number 13 is often considered lucky, contrary to many other cultures where it's seen as unlucky.

JOUR 16 : NOMBRES DE 11 À 20

1. Bonjour, combien sommes-nous dans la famille ?
2. la **mère**, le **père**, un **frère**, une **sœur** et moi.
3. Et combien de tasses de **thé** voulez-vous ?
4. **Onze**, s'il vous plaît. Pour tous nos amis aussi.
5. **Douze** bouteilles de **soda** aussi ?
6. Oui, et **treize** bouteilles d'**eau**.
7. Pour le **café**, combien ?
8. **Quatorze** tasses. Nous aimons beaucoup le café.
9. Et **quinze** canettes de **bière** pour finir ?

✤ In French, numbers from 11 to 20 are written as single words and used in the affirmative form just like in English, without any additional words needed.

DAY 16: NUMBERS FROM 11 TO 20

1. Hello, how many of us are in the family?
2. the **mother**, the **father**, a **brother**, a **sister**, and me.
3. And how many cups of **tea** would you like?
4. **Eleven**, please. For all our friends as well.
5. **Twelve** bottles of **soda** too?
6. Yes, and **thirteen** bottles of **water**.
7. For the **coffee**, how many?
8. **Fourteen** cups. We really like coffee.
9. And **fifteen** cans of **beer** to finish?

✤ In France, the nursery rhyme "Am Stram Gram" is used to choose someone randomly, similar to "Eeny, meeny, miny, moe," and involves counting to determine the selection.

1. Je veux **acheter** des fruits au **marché**.
2. Pourquoi ne pas aller au **magasin** ? Il y a une **réduction**.
3. Au **marché**, c'est plus **bon marché**. Et je préfère payer en **espèces**.
4. D'accord, mais regarde cette robe, elle est en **solde** !
5. C'est vrai, mais elle est encore trop **chère** pour moi.
6. Alors, utilisons ta **carte de crédit** ?
7. Non, je préfère **regarder** seulement aujourd'hui.

❖ To say you don't want something in French, use "ne...pas" around the verb, like "Je ne veux pas" for "I don't want."

1. I want to **buy** fruits at the **market**.
2. Why not go to the **store**? There's a **discount**.
3. At the **market**, it's cheaper. And I prefer to pay in **cash**.
4. Okay, but look at this dress, it's on **sale**!
5. That's true, but it's still too **expensive** for me.
6. So, shall we use your **credit card**?
7. No, I prefer to **look** only today.

✤ In traditional French markets, it's common to negotiate prices near closing time, often leading to delightful deals on fresh produce.

1. Bonjour, je cherche la **cabine d'essayage** pour ces **vêtements**.
2. C'est **tout droit**, puis à **gauche**.
3. Merci. Et où est la **caisse** ?
4. **Là-bas, à droite. Vous avez un panier ou un chariot** ?
5. Un **panier**. Combien coûtent ces **lunettes de soleil** ?
6. **Cinquante euros, mais il y a une réduction de dix** pour cent.
7. Super ! Et cette **veste** ?
8. **Cent euros, mais elle est en solde aussi. Vingt pour cent de réduction.**
9. Parfait, je prends les deux. Voici mon **reçu**.

✤ To ask how much something costs in French, use "Combien coûte...?" followed by the item.

1. Hello, I'm looking for the **fitting room** for these **clothes**.
2. It's **straight ahead**, then to the **left**.
3. Thank you. And where is the **cashier**?
4. **Over there, to the right. Do you have a basket or a cart?**
5. A **basket**. How much are these **sunglasses**?
6. **Fifty euros, but there's a discount of ten** percent.
7. Great! And this **jacket**?
8. **One hundred euros, but it's on sale too. Twenty percent off**.
9. Perfect, I'll take both. Here's my **receipt**.

❖ The world's first shopping mall, the "Passage du Caire," was established in Paris, France, in 1798, setting the stage for modern retail.

1. Bonjour, je voudrais aller à l'**aéroport**. Est-ce que je peux prendre un **taxi** ici ?
2. Oui, bien sûr. Le **taxi** est juste **à côté**.
3. Merci. Et combien ça coûte pour aller à l'**aéroport** ?
4. Ça coûte quinze euros.
5. C'est parfait. Et à l'**aéroport**, est-ce que je peux trouver un **bus** pour aller au **sud** ?
6. Oui, il y a un **bus** qui va au **sud** toutes les **douze** minutes.
7. Super ! Et pour le retour, est-il facile de trouver un **train** ou une **voiture** de location ?
8. Très facile. La **gare** est **derrière** l'**aéroport**, et il y a plusieurs agences de location de **voitures**.
9. Merci beaucoup pour votre aide.

✦ In French, to say "I take the bus," you use a declarative sentence: "Je prends le bus."

1. Hello, I would like to go to the **airport**. Can I take a **taxi** here?
2. Yes, of course. The **taxi** is right **next door**.
3. Thank you. And how much does it cost to go to the **airport**?
4. It costs fifteen euros.
5. That's perfect. And at the **airport**, can I find a **bus** to go **south**?
6. Yes, there's a **bus** that goes **south** every **twelve** minutes.
7. Great! And for the return, is it easy to find a **train** or a **rental car**?
8. Very easy. The **train station** is **behind** the **airport**, and there are several car rental agencies.
9. Thank you very much for your help.

✤ In Paris, there's a service called "Piscine-Bus" where a bus is converted into a mobile swimming pool, offering a refreshing commute during summer.

1. Bonjour, j'ai besoin d'**acheter** un **billet** de **train**, s'il vous plaît.
2. Bien sûr, **pourquoi** partez-vous ?
3. Je vais à l'**aéroport**. Mon vol **part** demain matin.
4. **Quand** voulez-vous partir ?
5. Le plus tôt possible, mais mon **train** est **retardé**.
6. Pas de problème. Voici votre **billet**. **Que** ferez-vous à l'**arrivée** ?
7. Je prendrai un **taxi** pour aller au **terminal**. J'ai une **valise** et un **sac à dos** comme **bagages**.
8. Parfait. La **porte** de **départ** est numéro 5. Bon voyage !
9. Merci beaucoup !

✤ To ask where someone is going in French, start with "Où vas-tu" for "Where are you going?"

1. Hello, I need to **buy** a **train ticket**, please.
2. Of course, **why** are you leaving?
3. I'm going to the **airport**. My flight **leaves** tomorrow morning.
4. **When** do you want to leave?
5. As soon as possible, but my **train** is **delayed**.
6. No problem. Here's your **ticket**. **What will you do upon arrival**?
7. I'll take a **taxi** to the **terminal**. I have a **suitcase** and a **backpack** as **luggage**.
8. Perfect. The **departure gate** is number 5. Have a good trip!
9. Thank you very much!

✤ In 1662, Paris introduced the world's first public bus service, initiated by Blaise Pascal.

CHALLENGE NO. 2

WRITE A SHORT TEXT IN FRENCH INTRODUCING YOURSELF AND EXPLAINING WHY YOU ARE LEARNING THIS LANGUAGE.

"Vivre, c'est apprendre."

"To live is to learn."

1. Bonjour, je cherche la **banque**. C'est loin d'ici ?
2. Non, c'est à côté de l'**hôpital**. Et toi, tu vas où ?
3. Je vais à la **pharmacie** maintenant, et après, à l'**école**.
4. Hier, j'étais au **restaurant** et au **bar**.
5. Ah bon ? Moi, demain, je vais à l'**hôtel**.
6. Après-demain, je veux aller au **parc**. Et toi ?
7. Moi, je travaille à la **maison** et au **bureau** toute la semaine.
8. C'est intéressant. J'aime bien aller au **parc** aussi.
9. Oui, c'est très agréable. Bonne journée !

✤ To give directions in French using the imperative, simply use the verb without a subject, like "Allez tout droit" for "Go straight ahead."

1. Hello, I'm looking for the **bank**. Is it far from here?
2. No, it's next to the **hospital**. And you, where are you going?
3. I'm going to the **pharmacy** now, and then to the **school**.
4. Yesterday, I was at the **restaurant** and the **bar**.
5. Oh really? Tomorrow, I'm going to the **hotel**.
6. The day after tomorrow, I want to go to the **park**. And you?
7. I work at **home** and at the **office** all week.
8. That's interesting. I like going to the **park** too.
9. Yes, it's very nice. Have a good day!

✤ France is home to Mont Saint-Michel, a breathtaking island commune that becomes isolated from the mainland during high tide, listed as a UNESCO World Heritage Site.

1. Ma **petite** maison est **basse** et **longue**. Et la tienne ?
2. Elle est **grande** et **large**, mais j'aime la tienne aussi.
3. Merci ! Tu vas à l'école **lundi** ?
4. Oui, en **bus**. C'est plus **lent** que la **voiture**, mais plus **rapide** que le **train**.
5. Moi, je prends mon **vélo**. C'est **fort** et **rapide** pour la ville.

❖ In French, to make an exclamatory sentence with an adjective, place "quel" or "quelle" before the noun it describes, matching the gender and number.

DAY 22: ADJECTIVES II

1. My **small** house is **low** and **long**. And yours?
2. It's **big** and **wide,** but I like yours too.
3. Thank you! Are you going to school on **Monday**?
4. Yes, by **bus**. It's slower than a **car,** but faster than a **train**.
5. I take my **bike**. It's **strong** and **fast** for the city.

✤ France's Mont Blanc, the highest peak in the Alps, is often called the "Roof of Europe."

1. Maman, pourquoi les **bagages** sont-ils si **lourds** ?
2. Parce qu'ils sont **pleins** de vêtements pour le **froid** et le **chaud**, mon chéri.
3. Et mon sac ? Il est très **léger**.
4. Oui, parce que tu as seulement tes jouets et quelques vêtements **doux**.
5. Papa, est-ce que le train est **retardé** ?
6. Non, il arrive à l'**heure**. Le **départ** est très **calme** aujourd'hui.
7. Super ! J'espère que le voyage ne sera pas trop **long**.
8. Ne t'inquiète pas. Avec toute la **famille** ensemble, le temps passera très **vite**.

✤ In French, to make a sentence negative, place "ne" before the verb and "pas" after it.

1. Mom, why are the **luggage** so **heavy**?
2. Because they are **full** of clothes for the **cold** and the **heat**, my dear.
3. And my bag? It's very **light**.
4. Yes, because you only have your toys and some **soft** clothes.
5. Dad, is the train **delayed**?
6. No, it's arriving **on time**. The **departure** is very **smooth** today.
7. Great! I hope the journey won't be too **long**.
8. Don't worry. With the whole **family** together, time will pass very **quickly**.

✤ French poets often use color adjectives uniquely, like "bleu outremer" (ultramarine blue), to evoke deep emotional landscapes.

1. J'aime le **bleu** et le **vert**, et toi ?
2. Moi, je préfère le **rouge** et le **jaune**. C'est plus **chaud**.
3. Ma **nièce** adore le **rose**. Elle dit que c'est une couleur **douce**.
4. Mon **cousin** aime le **noir**. Il trouve ça **cool**.
5. Et ton **oncle**, quelle est sa couleur préférée ?
6. Il aime le **marron** et le **gris**. C'est plus **calme** pour lui.
7. Ma **tante** a une **maison** avec des murs **blancs**. C'est très **froid**, je trouve.
8. Oui, mais avec des meubles **orange**, ça peut être joli.

✤ In French, the colors agree in gender and number with the noun they describe, so "blue" becomes "bleu" for a masculine noun and "bleue" for a feminine noun.

1. I like **blue** and **green**, what about you?
2. I prefer **red** and **yellow**. It's warmer.
3. My **niece** loves **pink**. She says it's a soft color.
4. My **cousin** likes **black**. He thinks it's **cool**.
5. And your **uncle**, what's his favorite color?
6. He likes **brown** and **gray**. It's calmer for him.
7. My **aunt** has a **house** with **white** walls. I find it very **cold**.
8. Yes, but with **orange** furniture, it can be pretty.

✤ In France, white is traditionally the color of royalty and purity, often seen in the elegant attire of French brides.

1. Bonjour, tu utilises quoi pour aller sur **Internet** ?
2. Salut, j'utilise mon **smartphone** et mon **ordinateur portable**. Et toi ?
3. Moi, je préfère mon **ordinateur**. C'est plus grand.
4. Tu reçois des **courriels** ?
5. Oui, beaucoup. Et je me connecte aux **réseaux sociaux** avec le **Wi-Fi**.
6. Tu as une **appli** préférée ?
7. Oui, j'utilise une **appli** pour **télécharger** des vidéos. Et toi, tu utilises quel **navigateur** ?
8. J'utilise le **navigateur** bleu. C'est rapide et facile.
9. Merci, au revoir !

✤ In French, always put a space before and after the colon (:) when writing about electronics and technology, like in "ordinateur portable : un outil essentiel".

DAY 25: ELECTRONICS AND TECHNOLOGY I 🌱

1. Hello, what do you use to go on **Internet**?
2. Hi, I use my **smartphone** and my **laptop**. And you?
3. I prefer my **computer**. It's bigger.
4. Do you get **emails**?
5. Yes, a lot. And I connect to **social networks** with **Wi-Fi**.
6. Do you have a favorite **app**?
7. Yes, I use an **app** to **download** videos. And you, which **browser** do you use?
8. I use the blue **browser**. It's fast and easy.
9. Thank you, goodbye!

✤ The French invented the hot air balloon in 1783, launching the first passengers, a sheep, a duck, and a rooster.

1. **Excusez-moi**, vous savez quel mois nous sommes ?
2. **Oui**, nous sommes en **septembre**.
3. Ah, et le temps, il est comment en **septembre** ?
4. Normalement, c'est assez **doux**. Pas trop **chaud**, pas trop **froid**.
5. **D'accord. Et en janvier** ?
6. En **janvier**, c'est très **froid**. **Février** et **mars** aussi.
7. **Peut-être** que je devrais visiter en **mai** ou **juin** alors.
8. **Oui**, c'est une bonne idée. **Juillet** et **août** sont très **chauds**.
9. Merci beaucoup pour votre aide.

✤ In French, to talk about events in past months or seasons, use the passé composé tense, like "J'ai visité Paris en juillet."

1. **Excuse me**, do you know what month it is?
2. **Yes**, we are in **September**.
3. Ah, and what's the weather like in **September**?
4. Normally, it's quite **mild**. Not too **hot**, not too **cold**.
5. **Alright. And in January**?
6. In **January**, it's very **cold**. **February** and **March** too.
7. **Maybe** I should visit in **May** or **June** then.
8. **Yes**, that's a good idea. **July** and **August** are very **hot**.
9. Thank you very much for your help.

✤ In France, the Fête de la Musique celebrates the summer solstice with free music performances across the country.

1. **Novembre** est un mois d'**automne**, tu sais.

2. Oui, et après vient **décembre**, le début de l'**hiver**.

3. Le **climat** change beaucoup avec les saisons. Les **prévisions** parlent de plus de **pluie** cet **hiver**.

4. J'aime quand il y a beaucoup d'**ensoleillement** au **printemps** et en **été**.

5. Moi aussi. Mais l'**automne** a de belles couleurs, et l'**hiver** est parfait pour le chocolat chaud.

6. C'est vrai. Chaque saison a quelque chose de spécial.

✤ To talk about future events happening in specific months or seasons in French, use the future tense of the verb "aller" (to go) followed by an infinitive verb, like "Je vais voyager en juillet." (I am going to travel in July).

1. **November** is an **autumn** month, you know.
2. Yes, and then comes **December**, the start of **winter**.
3. The **climate** changes a lot with the seasons. The **forecasts** are predicting more **rain** this **winter**.
4. I love it when there's a lot of **sunshine** in **spring** and **summer**.
5. Me too. But **autumn** has beautiful colors, and **winter** is perfect for hot chocolate.
6. That's true. Each season has something special.

✦ In France, the arrival of Beaujolais Nouveau wine is celebrated on the third Thursday of November, marking a festive tradition to welcome the wine season.

1. Bonjour, je suis **heureux** de te rencontrer. Comment **vas-tu** ?

2. Salut ! Je suis **joyeuse** aussi. Je **viens** de déménager ici. Et toi, tu **habites** ici depuis longtemps ?

3. Oui, depuis quelques années. Je suis **fier** de ma ville. Tu **fais** quoi dans la vie ?

4. Je travaille sur **internet**. Et toi ?

5. Je suis ingénieur en **informatique**. J'utilise beaucoup l'**ordinateur** et le **Wi-Fi**. Tu **aimes** les **réseaux sociaux** ?

6. Oui, ça me rend un peu **nerveuse** parfois, mais c'est **excitant**. Et toi, comment te sens-tu quand tu es **seul** ?

7. Quand je suis **seul**, je me sens un peu **triste**, mais je reste **détendu**. C'est important de se reposer.

8. Absolument. Enchanté de t'avoir rencontré.

9. Moi aussi, enchanté.

✤ The indicative mood is used to express facts and real situations, like "I am happy" or "She feels sad."

1. Hello, I am **happy** to meet you. How are **you**?
2. Hi! I'm **joyful** too. I **just** moved here. And you, have you **lived** here for a long time?
3. Yes, for a few years. I'm **proud** of my city. What do you **do** for a living?
4. I work on the **internet**. And you?
5. I'm a **computer** engineer. I use the **computer** and **Wi-Fi** a lot. Do you **like social media**?
6. Yes, it makes me a bit **nervous** sometimes, but it's **exciting**. And you, how do you feel when you're **alone**?
7. When I'm **alone**, I feel a bit **sad**, but I stay **relaxed**. It's important to rest.
8. Absolutely. Delighted to have met you.
9. Me too, delighted.

✦ In France, saying "I have the cockroach" ("J'ai le cafard") means feeling deeply sad or having the blues.

1. **Je suis stressé.** Demain, je vais à l'aéroport.
2. Pourquoi es-tu **confus** ?
3. Je ne sais pas si je dois prendre le **bus** ou un **taxi**.
4. **Je comprends. C'est toujours anxieux** de voyager.
5. Oui, et je suis un peu **contrarié. Tu vas me manquer** déjà.
6. Ne t'inquiète pas. **Je t'aime** et je serai **ravi** de te revoir en **mai**.
7. **Je suis heureux de l'entendre. Mais, je plaisante, je prends ma voiture.**
8. Ah, tu m'as **effrayé** ! **Je suis excité** pour toi.
9. Merci. **Tu vas** vraiment me manquer.

✤ Use the imperative mood to give commands or make requests, like "Souris!" which means "Smile!"

1. **I'm stressed**. Tomorrow, I'm going to the airport.
2. Why are you **confused**?
3. I don't know whether to take the **bus** or a **taxi**.
4. **I understand**. It's always **anxious** to travel.
5. Yes, and I'm a bit **upset**. **I'm going to miss you** already.
6. Don't worry. **I love you** and I'll be **delighted** to see you again in **May**.
7. **I'm happy to hear that. But, I'm joking, I'm taking my car**.
8. Ah, you **scared** me! **I'm excited** for you.
9. Thank you. **I'm** really going to miss you.

✤ Victor Hugo sent his wife a love poem every day for their entire marriage.

1. J'ai mal à la **tête** et mes **cheveux** sont en désordre.
2. Tu as quelque chose dans l'**œil** ? Et ton **oreille**, ça va ?
3. Oui, mais mon **nez** est bouché et ma **bouche** est sèche. Je pense que j'ai besoin d'**eau**.
4. Tu as mal aux **dents** aussi ?
5. Non, mes **dents** vont bien. Mais ma **main** et mon **bras** me font mal.
6. Et ta **jambe** ?
7. Ma **jambe** est OK. Je suis juste un peu stressé et confus avec le changement de **climat**.
8. Prends un peu de repos. Tu veux du **thé** ou du **café** ?
9. De l'**eau** suffira, merci.

✤ To express a wish or doubt about someone's body part, use the subjunctive mood after verbs like "vouloir que" or "douter que."

1. I have a **headache** and my **hair** is a mess.
2. Do you have something in your **eye**? And your **ear**, is it okay?
3. Yes, but my **nose** is blocked and my **mouth** is dry. I think I need some **water**.
4. Do your **teeth** hurt too?
5. No, my **teeth** are fine. But my **hand** and my **arm** hurt.
6. And your **leg**?
7. My **leg** is OK. I'm just a bit stressed and confused with the change in **climate**.
8. Take some rest. Would you like some **tea** or **coffee**?
9. **Water** will suffice, thank you.

✚ In France, the concept of "jolie laide" celebrates unconventional beauty, embracing flaws as attractive features.

CHALLENGE NO. 3

CHOOSE A SHORT ARTICLE IN A FRENCH NEWSPAPER AND TRANSLATE IT INTO ENGLISH.

"Bien dire fait rire, bien faire fait taire."

"Speaking well makes you laugh, doing well silences."

1. J'ai mal au **pied** et au **genou**. Peut-être parce que je suis tombé à l'**école**.

2. Oh, tu devrais mettre de la glace. Et comment va ton **dos** ?

3. Mon **dos** va bien, mais mon **cou** est un peu **froid**.

4. Tu as une écharpe pour ton **cou** ? Et ton **visage**, tu t'es fait mal ?

5. Non, mon **visage** et ma **peau** vont bien. Mais je me sens un peu **triste**.

6. Ne t'inquiète pas. On va à la **pharmacie** pour acheter quelque chose pour ton **pied** et ton **genou**.

7. Merci. J'espère que ça ira mieux **rapidement**. Je veux être **heureux** et **excité** pour le match demain.

8. Avec un peu de repos, ton **cerveau** et ton corps seront prêts. Tu seras **joyeux** demain, tu verras.

9. Oui, j'espère. Merci pour ton aide.

✤ If you wanted to say "I would have a headache if I read too much," in French, you would use the conditional mood: "J'aurais mal à la tête si je lisais trop."

1. I have a **foot** and **knee** pain. Maybe because I fell at **school**.
2. Oh, you should put some ice on it. And how is your **back**?
3. My **back** is fine, but my **neck** is a bit **cold**.
4. Do you have a scarf for your **neck**? And your **face**, did you hurt it?
5. No, my **face** and **skin** are fine. But I feel a bit **sad**.
6. Don't worry. We'll go to the **pharmacy** to buy something for your **foot** and **knee**.
7. Thank you. I hope it gets better **quickly**. I want to be **happy** and **excited** for the game tomorrow.
8. With a bit of rest, your **brain** and body will be ready. You'll be **joyful** tomorrow, you'll see.
9. Yes, I hope so. Thank you for your help.

✤ In Brittany, France, the traditional dance "Fest-Noz" is so culturally significant that it was UNESCO listed in 2012.

JOUR 32 : TEMPS ET CALENDRIER

1. Bonjour, peux-tu me donner l'**heure** ?
2. Oui, il est dix **heures** et une **minute**.
3. Merci. Et quel **jour** sommes-nous aujourd'hui ?
4. Nous sommes mercredi. Regarde le **calendrier** sur le mur.
5. Ah, d'accord. Et la **semaine** prochaine, tu es libre ?
6. Je dois regarder mon **emploi du temps**. Je pense que oui.
7. Super. Et sais-tu combien de **jours** il y a dans ce **mois** ?
8. Oui, il y a trente **jours** en avril.
9. Merci beaucoup. J'espère que cette **année** sera moins **stressante**.

✤ In French, to express an action happening at a specific time, use the active voice by placing the subject before the verb, as in "Je mange à midi" (I eat at noon).

1. Hello, can you tell me the **time**?
2. Yes, it is ten **hours** and one **minute**.
3. Thank you. And what **day** is it today?
4. It's Wednesday. Look at the **calendar** on the wall.
5. Ah, okay. And next **week**, are you free?
6. I need to check my **schedule**. I think so.
7. Great. And do you know how many **days** there are in this **month**?
8. Yes, there are thirty **days** in April.
9. Thank you very much. I hope this **year** will be less **stressful**.

✤ In France, the revolutionary calendar was used for 12 years, starting in 1793, renaming months to reflect nature, like Brumaire (Foggy) and Thermidor (Summer Heat).

1. Bonjour, tu veux du **thé** ou du **café** ce matin ?
2. Je préfère du **thé**, s'il te plaît. Et toi ?
3. Moi, je vais prendre un **café**. Pour le déjeuner, tu veux quoi ?
4. Hmm, peut-être de la **viande** avec des **légumes** et du **riz**.
5. Bonne idée ! J'ajouterai des **pâtes** aussi. Tu aimes les **œufs** ?
6. Oui, j'aime bien. Et comme **fruit**, on a des pommes.
7. Parfait. Il nous faut du **pain** aussi.
8. Oui, pour le petit déjeuner de demain. On a tout ce qu'il faut maintenant.
9. Super, allons préparer ça ensemble.

❖ In French, to form the passive voice, use "être" as the auxiliary verb followed by the past participle of the main verb, and agree the past participle with the subject.

1. Good morning, do you want **tea** or **coffee** this morning?
2. I'd prefer some **tea**, please. And you?
3. I'll have a **coffee**. What do you want for lunch?
4. Hmm, maybe some **meat** with **vegetables** and **rice**.
5. Good idea! I'll add some **pasta** too. Do you like **eggs**?
6. Yes, I like them. And for **fruit**, we have apples.
7. Perfect. We'll need some **bread** too.
8. Yes, for tomorrow's breakfast. We have everything we need now.
9. Great, let's go prepare it together.

✤ In France, the coq au vin recipe, a beloved national dish, was originally a way to tenderize tough roosters by slow-cooking them in wine.

1. **Qu'est-ce** que tu manges pour le déjeuner ?
2. Je mange un **sandwich** au **poulet** avec de la **salade** et du **fromage**. Et toi ?
3. Moi, je préfère une **soupe** de **légumes** avec un peu de **poivre** et de **beurre**.
4. **Quand est-ce que tu bois du café** ?
5. Je bois du **café** le matin. **Et** toi, **quand** bois-tu du **thé** ?
6. Je bois du **thé** l'après-midi. **Pourquoi** ne manges-tu pas de **viande** rouge comme le **bœuf** ou le **porc** ?
7. Je n'aime pas beaucoup la **viande** rouge. Je préfère le **poulet** ou les **légumes**.
8. **Comment** trouves-tu le **gâteau** au **chocolat** ?
9. C'est délicieux, surtout avec une touche de **crème** rouge sur le dessus.

✤ In French, to express with whom or with what you are eating, use the preposition "avec" followed by the noun, as in "Je mange avec une fourchette" (I eat with a fork).

1. **What** are you eating for lunch?
2. I'm having a **chicken sandwich** with **salad** and **cheese**. How about you?
3. I prefer a **vegetable soup** with a bit of **pepper** and **butter**.
4. **When do you drink coffee?**
5. I drink **coffee** in the morning. **And** you, **when do you drink tea?**
6. I drink **tea** in the afternoon. **Why** don't you eat red **meat** like **beef** or **pork?**
7. I'm not a big fan of red **meat**. I prefer **chicken** or **vegetables**.
8. **How do you find the chocolate cake?**
9. It's delicious, especially with a touch of red **cream** on top.

✤ The iconic French dish Coq au Vin was originally a way to tenderize tough roosters by slow-cooking them in wine.

1. Veux-tu un **soda** ou de l'**eau** ?
2. Je préfère du **jus**. Et toi ?
3. Moi, je vais prendre un verre de **vin**. Quel dessert choisis-tu ?
4. J'hésite entre une **glace** et une **tarte**.
5. Pourquoi pas une **pâtisserie** ? Ils ont de délicieux **chocolats**.
6. Bonne idée ! Et toi, que prends-tu ?
7. Je pense que je vais opter pour un **toast** au **fromage**.
8. Ça sonne bien. Après le repas, on pourrait aller prendre un café ?
9. Parfait ! J'adore passer du temps avec toi.

✦ In French, when talking about drinks and desserts, each item can be a subject in an independent clause, meaning it can stand alone as a complete sentence, like "Le café est chaud" (The coffee is hot).

1. Do you want a **soda** or some **water**?
2. I'd prefer some **juice**. How about you?
3. I'm going to have a glass of **wine**. Which dessert are you choosing?
4. I'm torn between **ice cream** and a **pie**.
5. Why not a **pastry**? They have delicious **chocolates**.
6. Good idea! And you, what will you have?
7. I think I'll go for a **cheese toast**.
8. Sounds good. After the meal, shall we go for a coffee?
9. Perfect! I love spending time with you.

✤ The Tarte Tatin was accidentally created by the Tatin sisters in France when one of them forgot to put the crust on their apple pie before baking.

1. Aujourd'hui, c'est **mercredi** et je veux préparer un dîner spécial.

2. Super, qu'as-tu en tête ?

3. Je pense à de la **viande rôtie et des légumes grillés.**

4. Ça sonne bien. Utiliseras-tu le **four** pour la viande ?

5. Oui, et je vais mettre les légumes au **réfrigérateur** pour qu'ils restent frais jusqu'à ce soir.

6. Parfait. Et pour boire ?

7. Peut-être du **vin**. Ça va bien avec la viande **rôtie**, tu ne trouves pas ?

8. Absolument. Et pour le dessert ?

9. Des fruits **cuits au four**. Simple mais délicieux.

✣ In French, when describing a recipe, use a subordinate clause starting with "que" to add details, like "Je veux que tu coupes les oignons." (I want you to chop the onions.)

1. Today is **Wednesday** and I want to prepare a special dinner.
2. Great, what do you have in mind?
3. I'm thinking of **roasted meat** and **grilled vegetables**.
4. That sounds good. Will you use the **oven** for the meat?
5. Yes, and I'm going to put the vegetables in the **refrigerator** to keep them fresh until tonight.
6. Perfect. And for drinks?
7. Maybe some **wine**. It goes well with **roasted** meat, don't you think?
8. Absolutely. And for dessert?
9. **Baked** fruits. Simple but delicious.

✤ Julia Child, an American chef, brought French cuisine to the American public, profoundly influencing home cooking in the United States.

1. J'aimerais aller à la **plage** cet **été** avec ma **famille**.
2. Moi, je préfère la **montagne**. Le **climat** est parfait au **printemps**.
3. Ma **sœur** adore la **forêt**. Elle aime faire des randonnées près de la **rivière**.
4. Mon **frère** veut explorer la **jungle**. Il trouve ça excitant.
5. Et nos parents ?
6. Notre **mère** rêve de visiter une **île** et notre **père** veut traverser le **désert**.
7. On pourrait aussi naviguer sur l'**océan** ou marcher dans une **vallée**.
8. Oui, chaque lieu a quelque chose d'unique. Mais après, on rentre à la maison pour un bon repas.
9. Exactement, avec du **poulet** et du **fromage**.

✤ In French, to create a complex sentence about travel and places, use "quand" (when) or "si" (if) to connect two ideas, like "Je visiterai Paris quand j'aurai des vacances" (I will visit Paris when I have vacation).

1. I'd like to go to the **beach** this **summer** with my **family**.
2. I prefer the **mountains**. The **climate** is perfect in **spring**.
3. My **sister** loves the **forest**. She enjoys hiking near the **river**.
4. My **brother** wants to explore the **jungle**. He finds it exciting.
5. And our parents?
6. Our **mother** dreams of visiting an **island** and our **father** wants to cross the **desert**.
7. We could also sail on the **ocean** or walk in a **valley**.
8. Yes, each place has something unique. But afterwards, we go home for a good meal.
9. Exactly, with some **chicken** and **cheese**.

✤ Victor Hugo often traveled with a piece of wood from Shakespeare's mulberry tree as a talisman.

1. **Bonjour, je suis à la plage et j'ai une** allergie au soleil. Que dois-je faire ?

2. **Prenez ce** médicament **et une** pilule toutes les quatre heures. Évitez le soleil.

3. **Merci. Et si j'ai une** blessure ?

4. **Allez à l'**hôpital **ou appelez la** police si c'est grave.

5. **Mon** cousin **s'est brûlé avec un** feu de camp.

6. **Il doit voir un** médecin **immédiatement. L'**hôpital peut aider.

7. **Ma** nièce a mal aux dents.

8. **Un** dentiste sera nécessaire. Prenez rendez-vous.

9. **Merci pour votre aide. Je me sens moins** nerveux maintenant.

✚ In French, adjectives change form to match the gender and number of the noun they describe, so for health emergencies, "un médecin compétent" becomes "une médecin compétente" for a skilled female doctor.

1. **Hello, I'm at the beach and I have a** sun allergy. What should I do?
2. **Take this** medicine **and a** pill every four hours. Avoid the sun.
3. **Thank you. And if I have an** injury?
4. **Go to the** hospital **or call the** police if it's serious.
5. **My** cousin **got burned by a** campfire.
6. **He needs to see a** doctor **immediately. The** hospital can help.
7. **My** niece has a toothache.
8. **A** dentist will be needed. Make an appointment.
9. **Thank you for your help. I feel less** nervous now.

✤ France's health system is so esteemed that it was ranked number 1 by the World Health Organization in 2000 for its overall performance.

1. J'ai **vingt-trois** ans et je suis **stressé**. J'ai eu un accident.

2. Oh non, as-tu une **blessure** ? Tu dois voir un **médecin**.

3. Oui, j'ai pris **trois médicaments** déjà. Le **médecin** dit que je vais mieux.

4. C'est bien. Tu as besoin de repos. Veux-tu quelque chose du **réfrigérateur** ?

5. Oui, peux-tu me donner **quatre** pommes ? Et **deux assiettes**, s'il te plaît.

6. Bien sûr. Voici les pommes et les **assiettes**. Tu veux une **cuillère** aussi ?

7. Non, merci. Je me sens un peu moins **anxieux** maintenant.

8. Bon, si tu as besoin de quelque chose, dis-le moi. Je suis là.

9. Merci beaucoup. Tu es un bon ami.

✤ In French, numbers 21-30 must agree in gender with the nouns they describe, except for 21, 31, etc., where "et un" or "et une" is used depending on the noun's gender.

1. I'm **twenty-three** years old and I'm **stressed**. I had an accident.
2. Oh no, do you have an **injury**? You need to see a **doctor**.
3. Yes, I've taken **three medications** already. The **doctor** says I'm getting better.
4. That's good. You need some rest. Do you want anything from the **refrigerator**?
5. Yes, can you give me **four** apples? And **two plates**, please.
6. Of course. Here are the apples and the **plates**. Do you want a **spoon** too?
7. No, thank you. I feel a bit less **anxious** now.
8. Good, if you need anything, let me know. I'm here.
9. Thank you so much. You're a good friend.

✤ In France, the first recorded lottery was organized in 1539 by King Francis I to help solve the kingdom's financial problems.

1. **Aujourd'hui**, c'est **lundi. Demain, ce sera mardi. Tu veux aller à la plage ou à la montagne ?**

2. **Mercredi**, j'ai prévu d'aller à la **forêt**. Mais **jeudi**, aller à la **mer** me semble une bonne idée.

3. **Vendredi**, je pense aller à la **rivière**. Et toi, que fais-tu **samedi** et **dimanche ?**

4. **Samedi, je vais me reposer. Dimanche, peut-être que je sortirai. J'aime sentir le vent dans mes cheveux et écouter la nature avec mes oreilles.**

5. Moi aussi. J'aime voir la beauté de la nature avec mes **yeux**. Et sentir l'air frais avec mon **nez**.

✤ In French, days of the week are not capitalized unless they start a sentence, and to compare two days, use "plus" for "more" and "moins" for "less."

1. **Today**, it's **Monday. Tomorrow, it will be Tuesday. Do you want to go to the beach or to the mountains**?
2. **Wednesday**, I plan to go to the **forest**. But **Thursday**, going to the **sea** seems like a good idea.
3. **Friday**, I'm thinking of going to the **river**. And you, what are you doing **Saturday** and **Sunday**?
4. **Saturday**, I'm going to rest. **Sunday**, maybe I'll go out. I like feeling the wind in my **hair** and listening to nature with my **ears**.
5. Me too. I love seeing the beauty of nature with my **eyes**. And smelling the fresh air with my **nose**.

✤ In France, Tuesday the 13th is considered unlucky, not Friday the 13th, due to the belief that Tuesday is dominated by Mars, the god of war.

CHALLENGE NO. 4

WRITE A LETTER OR EMAIL IN FRENCH TO A FICTIONAL OR REAL FRIEND.

"Chaque langue est un univers."

"Every language is a universe."

125

JOUR 41 : NETTOYAGE I 🌱

1. Aujourd'hui, c'est lundi, je vais nettoyer la **salle de bain** et la **cuisine**.
2. Bonne idée ! Moi, je vais m'occuper de la **table** et des **chaises** dans le salon.
3. Est-ce que tu peux aussi dépoussiérer la **lampe** et les **fenêtres** ?
4. Bien sûr ! Et toi, peux-tu vérifier si la **porte** du **salon** ferme bien ?
5. Oui, je le ferai. Après, je pense qu'il faudra passer l'aspirateur près du **lit** et le long des **murs**.
6. D'accord. Ensuite, on prendra un **apéritif** pour célébrer notre travail.
7. Parfait ! Un nettoyage efficace et une petite récompense après.

❖ In French, to form the superlative of adjectives, you add "le/la/les plus" before the adjective for "the most" and "le/la/les moins" before the adjective for "the least."

1. Today is Monday, I'm going to clean the **bathroom** and the **kitchen**.
2. Good idea! I'll take care of the **table** and **chairs** in the living room.
3. Can you also dust the **lamp** and the **windows**?
4. Of course! And can you check if the **door** to the **living room** closes properly?
5. Yes, I'll do that. After, I think we'll need to vacuum near the **bed** and along the **walls**.
6. Alright. Then, we'll have an **aperitif** to celebrate our work.
7. Perfect! Efficient cleaning and a little reward afterward.

✤ In France, the grand spring cleaning tradition is known as "le grand nettoyage de printemps," where homes are thoroughly cleaned from top to bottom to welcome the new season.

1. Aujourd'hui, je nettoie ma **maison**. Et toi ?
2. Moi, je m'occupe de mon **appartement**. Je commence par le **toit**.
3. Le **toit** ? C'est original. Moi, je fais chaque **pièce**.
4. J'ai un petit **jardin** et un **garage** à ranger aussi.
5. Chanceux ! Je n'ai qu'un **balcon**. Mais, je vais nettoyer les **escaliers**.
6. Ah, tu vis en **étage** ?
7. Oui, au vingt-troisième. Et toi ?
8. Au rez-de-chaussée. Aujourd'hui, je nettoie surtout le **plafond** de la **cuisine**.
9. Bon courage ! Moi, je finis avec les **vêtements** puis je me repose.

✤ In French, to compare two things, use "plus... que" for "more... than", "moins... que" for "less... than", and "aussi... que" for "as... as".

1. Today, I'm cleaning my **house**. And you?
2. Me, I'm taking care of my **apartment**. I'm starting with the **roof**.
3. The **roof**? That's original. I do each **room**.
4. I have a small **garden** and a **garage** to tidy up as well.
5. Lucky! I only have a **balcony**. But, I'm going to clean the **stairs**.
6. Oh, you live on an **upper floor**?
7. Yes, on the twenty-third. And you?
8. On the ground floor. Today, I'm mainly cleaning the **ceiling** of the **kitchen**.
9. Good luck! I'm finishing with the **clothes** then I'm resting.

✤ The French Revolution sparked not just political change but also domestic innovation, leading to the creation of the first mechanical refrigerator by a French monk in 1805.

1. Bonjour, peux-tu me dire où est le jardin ?
2. Oui, le jardin est **à l'arrière** de la **maison, entre le garage et le potager**.
3. Merci. Et où puis-je trouver du thé ?
4. Le thé est **à l'intérieur, à côté de la cuisine, ici**.
5. Super. Est-ce que le bus pour l'aéroport passe **ici** ou **là** ?
6. Il passe **à gauche** de la **maison, là**.
7. Et quand est le prochain bus ?
8. **Mercredi, à l'heure**.
9. Merci beaucoup pour ton aide.

✤ In French, to express going to a specific place, use "aller à" followed by the location, but for going to a country or continent, use "aller en" if it's feminine and "aller au" if it's masculine.

DAY 43: DIRECTION AND LOCATION II

1. Hello, can you tell me where the garden is?
2. Yes, the garden is **at the back** of the **house, between the garage and the vegetable garden**.
3. Thank you. And where can I find some tea?
4. The tea is **inside, next to the kitchen, here**.
5. Great. Does the bus to the airport pass **here** or **there**?
6. It passes **to the left** of the **house, there**.
7. And when is the next bus?
8. **Wednesday, on time**.
9. Thank you very much for your help.

✢ French cartographer Martin Waldseemüller was the first to name the newly discovered continent "America" in 1507, after explorer Amerigo Vespucci.

1. Bonjour, je cherche le **centre commercial**.
2. C'est à **droite**, près de l'**épicerie**.
3. Merci. J'ai besoin d'un **panier** pour mes achats.
4. À la **caisse**, vous pouvez demander un **remboursement** si le **prix** ne vous convient pas.
5. Super, et il y a des **réductions** aujourd'hui ?
6. Oui, il y a un grand **solde** sur le **fromage** et le **poulet**.
7. Parfait. Vous savez où je peux trouver le **beurre** ?
8. **Ici, près de la porte. N'oubliez pas votre reçu** pour le **remboursement**.
9. Merci beaucoup pour votre aide.

✤ In French, when asking a question, especially about shopping, you often invert the subject and the verb, like "Achète-t-il un manteau?" (Is he buying a coat?).

DAY 44: SHOPPING III 🌱

1. Hello, I'm looking for the **shopping center**.
2. It's to the **right**, near the **grocery store**.
3. Thank you. I need a **basket** for my shopping.
4. At the **checkout**, you can ask for a **refund** if the **price** is not right for you.
5. Great, and are there any **discounts** today?
6. Yes, there's a big **sale** on **cheese** and **chicken**.
7. Perfect. Do you know where I can find the **butter**?
8. **Here, near the door. Don't forget your receipt** for the **refund**.
9. Thank you very much for your help.

✤ In France, it's considered polite to open a gift immediately upon receiving it to express gratitude and appreciation to the giver.

1. Bonjour, je voudrais **acheter** du lait et du jus, s'il vous plaît.
2. Bien sûr, cela fera 5 euros. Vous payez comment ?
3. Je vais utiliser ma **carte de débit**. Je n'ai pas assez d'**espèces**.
4. D'accord. Insérez votre carte, s'il vous plaît. Vous avez besoin d'autre chose ?
5. Oui, avez-vous aussi du soda en **réduction** ?
6. Oui, nous avons une **réduction** de 10% sur les sodas aujourd'hui.
7. Parfait, j'en prendrai deux. Et voilà, c'est payé.
8. Merci beaucoup. Vous voulez un **reçu** ?
9. Non, c'est bon. Merci et au revoir.

✤ In French, the currency symbol comes after the amount, unlike in English.

1. Hello, I would like to **buy** some milk and juice, please.
2. Of course, that will be 5 euros. How will you be paying?
3. I'll use my **debit card**. I don't have enough **cash**.
4. Alright. Please insert your card. Do you need anything else?
5. Yes, do you also have soda on **sale**?
6. Yes, we have a 10% **discount** on sodas today.
7. Perfect, I'll take two. And there, it's paid.
8. Thank you very much. Would you like a **receipt**?
9. No, that's fine. Thank you and goodbye.

✤ In 1360, France created the franc, named after King John II, who was freed from English captivity for a ransom of 3 million crowns.

1. Aujourd'hui, le **climat** est comment ?
2. La **prévision** dit qu'il sera **humide** avec du **tonnerre** et un **éclair**.
3. Oh, et après la pluie, on verra un **arc-en-ciel** ?
4. Oui, et peut-être une petite **bruine** mais sans **flocon de neige**.
5. J'espère qu'il y aura un peu d'**ensoleillement**.
6. Moi aussi. Mais avec tous ces **nuages**, c'est difficile.
7. Au moins, l'**arc-en-ciel** rendra le ciel beau.
8. Exactement. J'aime quand la nature nous montre sa beauté.
9. Moi aussi. C'est magnifique, n'est-ce pas ?

❖ In French, to describe the weather, we often use the verb "faire" as in "Il fait chaud" (It is hot), and for natural phenomena, we use "Il y a" like in "Il y a du vent" (There is wind).

DAY 46: WEATHER AND NATURE

1. Today, what's the **weather** like?
2. The **forecast** says it will be **humid** with **thunder** and **lightning**.
3. Oh, and after the rain, will we see a **rainbow**?
4. Yes, and maybe a little **drizzle** but no **snowflakes**.
5. I hope there will be some **sunshine**.
6. Me too. But with all these **clouds**, it's difficult.
7. At least the **rainbow** will make the sky beautiful.
8. Exactly. I love it when nature shows us its beauty.
9. Me too. It's magnificent, isn't it?

✤ In France, it's believed that the mysterious Brocéliande Forest is the home of the legendary wizard Merlin from Arthurian legend.

1. Hier, il y avait une **tempête** très forte près de la **montagne**.

2. Oui, et j'ai entendu qu'un **ouragan** approchait de la **mer**.

3. C'est effrayant ! La dernière fois, une **tornade** a détruit le **centre commercial**.

4. Vraiment ? Et le **tremblement de terre** l'année dernière a ouvert un **canyon** près de la **rivière**.

5. J'espère que le **climat** sera plus **calme** cette semaine. J'ai vu la **prévision**.

6. Moi aussi. J'aime quand il fait **chaud** et **doux**, pas **humide** avec du **tonnerre**.

7. On pourrait aller à l'**étang** ou explorer une **grotte** si le temps le permet.

8. Bonne idée ! Et peut-être que le **supermarché** aura une **réduction** sur les équipements.

9. Oui, après tout ça, un peu de **calme** serait bien.

✤ In French, the final consonants of most geographical names and disaster-related words are silent, except when the next word starts with a vowel, causing a liaison.

1. Yesterday, there was a very strong **storm** near the **mountain**.
2. Yes, and I heard that a **hurricane** was approaching the **sea**.
3. That's scary! Last time, a **tornado** destroyed the **shopping mall**.
4. Really? And the **earthquake** last year opened up a **canyon** near the **river**.
5. I hope the **weather** will be more **calm** this week. I saw the **forecast**.
6. Me too. I like it when it's **warm** and **gentle**, not **humid** with **thunder**.
7. We could go to the **pond** or explore a **cave** if the weather allows.
8. Good idea! And maybe the **supermarket** will have a **discount** on gear.
9. Yes, after all that, a bit of **peace** would be nice.

✤ In France, the legend of the sunken city of Ys claims it was swallowed by the ocean as divine punishment for its sinfulness.

1. Quelle est ta couleur préférée ?
2. J'aime beaucoup le **bleu** et le **vert**.
3. Moi, je préfère le **rouge** et le **jaune**. Et le **noir**, tu aimes ?
4. Oui, le **noir** est élégant. Mais le **blanc** est aussi très beau.
5. C'est vrai. Et le **rose** ?
6. Le **rose** est doux, mais je n'aime pas trop le **marron**.
7. Moi non plus. Et le **gris** ?
8. Le **gris** est joli. Et l'**or** ?
9. L'**or** est magnifique, très spécial.

✤ In French, the final consonant of a color adjective is not pronounced unless it comes before a noun that begins with a vowel or is in the plural form.

1. What's your favorite color?
2. I really like **blue** and **green**.
3. I prefer **red** and **yellow**. And **black**, do you like it?
4. Yes, **black** is elegant. But **white** is also very beautiful.
5. That's true. And **pink**?
6. **Pink is soft, but I don't really like brown**.
7. Me neither. And **gray**?
8. **Gray is pretty. And gold**?
9. **Gold** is magnificent, very special.

✤ In France, the Fête du Citron (Lemon Festival) in Menton dazzles with vibrant yellow and orange citrus sculptures.

1. As-tu **internet** sur ton **smartphone** ?
2. Oui, et j'utilise le **Wi-Fi** pour me connecter. Et toi, tu utilises ton **ordinateur** ?
3. Moi, j'ai un **ordinateur portable**. Je préfère envoyer des **courriels** et naviguer sur les **réseaux sociaux**.
4. Tu as une **appli** préférée sur ton **smartphone** ?
5. Oui, j'utilise une **appli** pour **télécharger** des livres. Et toi, quel **navigateur** utilises-tu ?
6. J'utilise le plus souvent Chrome. C'est rapide pour **télécharger** des vidéos.

❖ In French, stress always falls on the last syllable of a word, making it sound slightly longer and louder.

1. Do you have **internet** on your **smartphone**?
2. Yes, and I use **Wi-Fi** to connect. What about you, do you use your **computer**?
3. I have a **laptop**. I prefer to send **emails** and browse **social networks**.
4. Do you have a favorite **app** on your **smartphone**?
5. Yes, I use an **app** to **download** books. And you, which **browser** do you use?
6. I mostly use Chrome. It's fast for **downloading** videos.

✤ In 1631, France launched its first regular newspaper, La Gazette, marking the beginning of organized news distribution.

1. As-tu vu les **actualités** à la **télévision** hier soir ?
2. Non, j'ai écouté la **radio**. Ils parlaient d'une **tempête**.
3. Ah, j'ai utilisé mon **smartphone** pour voir les infos sur les **réseaux sociaux**. Il y avait aussi des alertes sur un **tremblement de terre**.
4. Vraiment ? J'ai perdu mon **mot de passe** et mon **nom d'utilisateur** pour me connecter.
5. Tu devrais noter ton **mot de passe** quelque part. Au fait, as-tu vu ma nouvelle **imprimante** ?
6. Oui, elle est près de ton **ordinateur**. Et ton **appareil photo**, tu l'as utilisé récemment ?
7. Pas encore. Mais je vais prendre des photos ce **vendredi**.

✤ In French, accents like é (acute accent) can change the meaning of a word, for example, "e" means "and," but "é" (as in "téléphone") changes the sound to "ay" and often indicates past tense or emphasis in technology terms.

1. Did you see the **news** on **TV** last night?
2. No, I listened to the **radio**. They were talking about a **storm**.
3. Ah, I used my **smartphone** to check the news on **social media**. There were also alerts about an **earthquake**.
4. Really? I lost my **password** and **username** to log in.
5. You should write down your **password** somewhere. By the way, have you seen my new **printer**?
6. Yes, it's next to your **computer**. And your **camera**, have you used it recently?
7. Not yet. But I'm going to take some pictures this **Friday**.

✤ In France, the Yellow Vest protests, initially sparked by fuel tax hikes, were largely organized and amplified through social media platforms.

CHALLENGE NO. 5

LISTEN TO A PODCAST IN FRENCH AND SUMMARIZE IT, IN WRITING OR ORALLY.

"**La curiosité mène à tout : parfois à écouter aux portes,** *parfois à* **découvrir l'Amérique.**"
"Curiosity leads to everything: sometimes to eavesdropping, sometimes to discovering America."

1. J'ai un nouvel **animal**. C'est un **chat** noir.
2. Oh, j'adore les **chats** ! J'ai un **chien** et un **oiseau** bleu.
3. Mon frère veut un **poisson** rouge. Et toi, tu aimes les **chevaux** ?
4. Oui, mais je préfère les **vaches** et les **cochons**. Les **souris**, pas trop.
5. Moi, j'ai peur des **souris**. Et les **poulets**, tu aimes ?
6. Oui, surtout au printemps. Le **climat** est parfait pour aller à la ferme.
7. C'est vrai. Au printemps, tout est vert et beau.

✤ In French, to say "the cat and the dog," we link the words by saying "le chat et le chien," using "et" for "and."

1. I have a new **animal**. It's a black **cat**.
2. Oh, I love **cats**! I have a **dog** and a blue **bird**.
3. My brother wants a goldfish. And you, do you like **horses**?
4. Yes, but I prefer **cows** and **pigs**. Not so much **mice**.
5. I'm scared of **mice**. And **chickens**, do you like them?
6. Yes, especially in the spring. The **weather** is perfect for going to the farm.
7. That's true. In the spring, everything is green and beautiful.

✤ The Gallic Rooster became France's national symbol due to a Latin pun between "gallus" (rooster) and "Gallus" (Gallic).

JOUR 52 : LES PLANTES ET LA NATURE

1. J'aime beaucoup les **plantes** et la **nature**. Et toi ?
2. Oui, moi aussi. J'adore marcher dans la **forêt** et voir les **arbres** et les **fleurs**.
3. Hier, j'ai vu un **oiseau** sur une **feuille**. C'était très **joyeux**.
4. Moi, j'ai un **jardin** à la **maison**. Il y a beaucoup d'**herbe** et quelques **arbres**.
5. C'est beau ! Tu as des **animaux** dans ton jardin ?
6. Juste un **chat**. Il aime dormir sous les **arbres**.
7. La **nature** me rend toujours **heureuse**. Et l'**océan**, tu aimes ?
8. Oui, l'**océan** et la **rivière** sont magnifiques. Mais je n'aime pas trop la **jungle** ou la **montagne**.
9. Moi, je trouve que chaque partie de la nature a quelque chose de spécial.

✤ In French, before a vowel or mute 'h', "le" and "la" become "l'" to make speaking smoother, like in "l'arbre" (the tree).

DAY 52: PLANTS AND NATURE

1. I really like **plants** and **nature**. How about you?
2. Yes, me too. I love walking in the **forest** and seeing the **trees** and **flowers**.
3. Yesterday, I saw a **bird** on a **leaf**. It was very **joyful**.
4. I have a **garden** at **home**. There's a lot of **grass** and a few **trees**.
5. That's beautiful! Do you have any **animals** in your garden?
6. Just a **cat**. It likes to sleep under the **trees**.
7. **Nature** always makes me **happy**. And the **ocean**, do you like it?
8. Yes, the **ocean** and the **river** are beautiful. But I'm not too fond of the **jungle** or the **mountains**.
9. I think every part of nature has something special.

✤ In France, lavender has been used for centuries not just for its pleasant scent but also for its healing properties, particularly in treating insomnia and anxiety.

1. J'ai **trente et un** arbres dans mon jardin.

2. Vraiment ? Moi, j'ai **trente-deux** fleurs près de la rivière.

3. Hier, j'ai vu **trente-trois** oiseaux dans la forêt. C'était beau.

4. J'écoute souvent les actualités sur la radio, il y avait **trente-quatre** nouvelles importantes.

5. Sur ma télévision, il y a **trente-cinq** chaînes, mais je regarde seulement quelques-unes.

6. Tu utilises la télécommande pour changer de chaîne ?

7. Oui, mais parfois je suis confus et je pousse le bouton **haut** au lieu de **bas**.

8. Moi, je me sens stressé quand je ne trouve pas la télécommande.

9. Hier, j'étais effrayé parce que j'ai entendu un bruit à **minuit**.

✤ In French, when counting from 31 to 40, we use "trente-et-un" for 31 but just add the number for the rest, like "trente-deux" for 32, without any contraction.

1. I have **thirty-one** trees in my garden.
2. Really? I have **thirty-two** flowers near the river.
3. Yesterday, I saw **thirty-three** birds in the forest. It was beautiful.
4. I often listen to the news on the radio, there were **thirty-four** important news items.
5. On my television, there are **thirty-five** channels, but I only watch a few of them.
6. Do you use the remote to change the channel?
7. Yes, but sometimes I get confused and press the **up** button instead of **down**.
8. I feel stressed when I can't find the remote.
9. Yesterday, I was scared because I heard a noise at **midnight**.

✤ The Eiffel Tower, a symbol of French architecture, has 1,665 steps to the top.

1. J'aime beaucoup la **musique**. Et toi, tu préfères quelle **chanson** ?
2. Ma **chanson** préférée est chantée par mon **chanteur** favori. Il joue dans un **groupe** connu.
3. Moi, j'adore aller au **théâtre** et regarder des **films**. Mais écouter la **radio** et **danser** me plaît aussi.
4. As-tu déjà assisté à un **concert** ?
5. Oui, c'était incroyable ! Le **groupe** jouait si bien. La **danse** et la **musique** étaient parfaites.
6. J'aimerais voir plus de **concerts**. La **musique** en direct a quelque chose de spécial.
7. Absolument. Rien ne vaut l'expérience de voir ton **chanteur** ou **chanteuse** préféré(e) en personne.

✤ In French, when talking about music and entertainment, use the definite article (le, la, les) to talk about genres or specific works, like "Le jazz est amusant" (Jazz is fun).

1. I really like **music**. And you, which **song** do you prefer?
2. My favorite **song** is sung by my favorite **singer**. He plays in a well-known **band**.
3. I love going to the **theater** and watching **movies**. But listening to the **radio** and **dancing** also pleases me.
4. Have you ever been to a **concert**?
5. Yes, it was incredible! The **band** played so well. The **dance** and the **music** were perfect.
6. I would like to see more **concerts**. Live **music** has something special about it.
7. Absolutely. Nothing beats the experience of seeing your favorite **singer** or **singer** in person.

♣ In Brittany, France, the binioù kozh, an ancient form of bagpipe, is traditionally paired with the bombarde, a type of oboe, to create a uniquely Breton sound.

1. Je vais à l'**aéroport** pour prendre un **avion**.
2. Pourquoi pas le **train** ou le **bus** ?
3. C'est plus rapide en **avion**. Et toi, tu préfères la **voiture** ou le **taxi** ?
4. Moi, j'aime bien le **vélo**. Mais pour aller loin, je prends le **bateau** depuis le **port**.
5. Ah, c'est intéressant. Et tu achètes tes billets à la **gare** ou en ligne ?
6. En ligne, c'est plus facile pour **acheter** et **vendre**.
7. Tu as raison. Moi, j'ai mal au **pied** quand je marche trop.
8. Moi, c'est le **dos**. Voyager en **avion** me repose.
9. Oui, c'est confortable et on arrive vite.

✤ In French, to express "some" or "any" when talking about transportation, use "des" before plural nouns and "de" before singular nouns that start with a vowel or silent 'h'.

1. I'm going to the **airport** to catch a **plane**.
2. Why not take the **train** or the **bus**?
3. It's faster by **plane**. And you, do you prefer the **car** or the **taxi**?
4. Me, I really like the **bicycle**. But for going far, I take the **boat** from the **port**.
5. Ah, that's interesting. And do you buy your tickets at the **station** or online?
6. Online, it's easier to **buy** and **sell**.
7. You're right. I get a sore **foot** when I walk too much.
8. For me, it's my **back**. Traveling by **plane** gives me a rest.
9. Yes, it's comfortable and you get there quickly.

♣ In the 18th century, French explorers like La Salle claimed vast territories in North America, dreaming of a French empire that stretched from the Great Lakes to the Gulf of Mexico.

1. Aujourd'hui, je vais au **centre commercial** pour acheter des **vêtements**.
2. Ah bon ? Moi, je cherche une **veste** et des **bijoux**.
3. Tu devrais regarder les **boucles d'oreilles** et les **colliers** en **solde**.
4. Oui, j'espère trouver une bonne **réduction**. Tu sais si c'est ouvert toute la **semaine** ?
5. Normalement, oui. Mais vérifie les **prévisions** climatiques, il va être **humide** avec du **tonnerre**.
6. D'accord, je prendrai mon parapluie. Et après, je dois aller à l'**épicerie**.
7. Moi aussi. J'espère qu'ils auront ce que je cherche.
8. Bon shopping alors !
9. Merci, à toi aussi !

✤ To show something belongs to someone in French, add an apostrophe and "s" to the owner's name if it ends in a vowel, or just an "s" if it ends in a consonant, like "Marie's book" becomes "le livre de Marie."

DAY 56: SHOPPING II ✂

1. Today, I'm going to the **mall** to buy some **clothes**.
2. Oh really? I'm looking for a **jacket** and some **jewelry**.
3. You should check out the **earrings** and **necklaces** on **sale**.
4. Yes, I hope to find a good **discount**. Do you know if it's open all **week**?
5. Normally, yes. But check the **weather forecast**, it's going to be **humid** with **thunder**.
6. Alright, I'll take my umbrella. And afterwards, I need to go to the **grocery store**.
7. Me too. I hope they have what I'm looking for.
8. Happy shopping then!
9. Thanks, you too!

✤ In France, the world's largest flea market, La Braderie de Lille, transforms the city into a treasure hunter's paradise every September.

JOUR 57 : CORPS ET SANTÉ II

1. J'ai mal au **dos** et aux **jambes** après le concert hier.
2. Moi, j'ai mal à la **tête**. La musique était très forte.
3. Oui, et le **chanteur** était incroyable, n'est-ce pas ?
4. Absolument, et j'ai adoré le **groupe**. Tu veux du **thé** ou du **café** maintenant ?
5. Un **thé**, s'il te plaît. Mes **oreilles** ont besoin de repos.
6. D'accord. Et après, on pourrait aller au supermarché. Il y a des **soldes** sur les **légumes**.
7. Bonne idée. J'ai besoin de manger sain pour ma **santé**.
8. Exactement. Et peut-être un peu de **viande** pour le dîner ?
9. Oui, et n'oublions pas de vérifier nos **dents** après tout ce sucre hier soir.

✤ This shirt hurts my arm: Cette chemise me fait mal au bras.

1. I have a sore **back** and **legs** after the concert yesterday.
2. I have a headache. The music was very loud.
3. Yes, and the **singer** was incredible, wasn't he?
4. Absolutely, and I loved the **band**. Do you want some **tea** or **coffee** now?
5. A **tea**, please. My **ears** need a rest.
6. Alright. And afterwards, we could go to the supermarket. There are **sales** on **vegetables**.
7. Good idea. I need to eat healthy for my **health**.
8. Exactly. And maybe a bit of **meat** for dinner?
9. Yes, and let's not forget to check our **teeth** after all that sugar last night.

♣ In France, the town of Vichy is famed for its healing thermal waters, attracting visitors since Roman times for their medicinal properties.

1. Bonjour, je suis **médecin**. J'aide les gens qui ont mal à la **tête** ou à la **jambe**.

2. Moi, je suis **dentiste**. Je soigne les dents.

3. Et moi, **avocat**. Je travaille au tribunal.

4. Je suis **enseignante**. J'enseigne à l'école.

5. Moi, **serveuse** dans un restaurant. Je sers du **poulet** et du **bœuf**.

6. Je suis le **chef** ici. J'aime cuisiner avec du **beurre** et du **fromage**.

7. En tant que **directrice**, je gère l'entreprise.

8. Je suis **présidente** d'une grande société. Je voyage souvent en **avion** ou en **voiture**.

9. Et moi, **auteure**. J'écris des livres.

✤ In French, to describe a profession someone has, we use "qui" as a relative pronoun without an article, like in "Elle est une avocate qui travaille à Paris" (She is a lawyer who works in Paris).

1. Hello, I am a **doctor**. I help people who have a headache or a leg ache.
2. Me, I'm a **dentist**. I treat teeth.
3. And me, a **lawyer**. I work in court.
4. I am a **teacher**. I teach at school.
5. Me, a **waitress** in a restaurant. I serve **chicken** and **beef**.
6. I am the **chef** here. I like to cook with **butter** and **cheese**.
7. As a **director**, I manage the company.
8. I am the **president** of a large company. I often travel by **plane** or **car**.
9. And me, an **author**. I write books.

✤ In France, the art of creating delicate lace by hand, known as "Dentelle," dates back to the 16th century and is still practiced in regions like Alençon, renowned for its exquisite craftsmanship.

1. J'ai acheté un **four** et un **réfrigérateur** pour ma cuisine hier.
2. Vraiment ? Moi, j'ai trouvé une belle **lampe** pour ma **table** et deux **chaises**.
3. Et pour le salon ?
4. J'ai choisi un **canapé** confortable et mis une **table basse** près de la **porte**.
5. Tu as vu l'**horloge** en solde au supermarché ?
6. Oui, mais je n'avais pas assez d'argent après avoir acheté tous ces articles ménagers.
7. C'est dommage. Les soldes sont une bonne occasion pour économiser.
8. Exactement. La prochaine fois, j'irai plus tôt.

✚ In French, to talk about an indefinite amount of household items, use "des" before the noun, like "des chaises" for "chairs."

1. I bought an **oven** and a **refrigerator** for my kitchen yesterday.
2. Really? I found a beautiful **lamp** for my **table** and two **chairs**.
3. And for the living room?
4. I chose a comfortable **sofa** and placed a **coffee table** near the **door**.
5. Did you see the **clock** on sale at the supermarket?
6. Yes, but I didn't have enough money after buying all those household items.
7. That's a shame. Sales are a good opportunity to save.
8. Exactly. Next time, I'll go earlier.

✤ The French invented the stethoscope in 1816, revolutionizing medical diagnostics.

1. Quelle est la **taille** de ton nouveau **réfrigérateur** ?
2. Il a une **hauteur** de deux **mètres**, une **largeur** de soixante **centimètres** et une **profondeur** de soixante-dix **centimètres**.
3. Et le **poids** ?
4. Environ soixante **kilogrammes**.
5. Impressionnant ! Et ta nouvelle **télévision**, quelle est sa **taille** ?
6. Elle a une **diagonale** de cinquante **pouces**.
7. Tu as aussi acheté un nouveau **lit** ?
8. Oui, il a une **longueur** de deux **mètres** et une **largeur** d'un **mètre** et demi. Très confortable pour mes **jambes** et mon **dos** !

✤ In French, to describe an ongoing action related to measurements or size, use the present participle by adding "-ant" to the verb, like "mesurant" for "measuring."

1. What is the **size** of your new **refrigerator**?
2. It has a **height** of two **meters**, a **width** of sixty **centimeters**, and a **depth** of seventy **centimeters**.
3. And the **weight**?
4. About sixty **kilograms**.
5. Impressive! And your new **television**, what is its **size**?
6. It has a **diagonal** of fifty **inches**.
7. Did you also buy a new **bed**?
8. Yes, it has a **length** of two **meters** and a **width** of one and a half **meters**. Very comfortable for my **legs** and **back**!

✤ In ancient France, the length of a foot varied from region to region until the metric system was introduced.

CHALLENGE NO. 6

RECORD A SHORT AUDIO WHERE YOU TALK ABOUT YOUR PROGRESS IN FRENCH.

"Toutes les cultures sont des fenêtres ouvertes sur le *monde.*"

"All cultures are windows open to the world."

1. Aujourd'hui, je vais préparer des **pâtes** avec du **beurre** et du **poivre**.

2. Oh, j'aime beaucoup les **pâtes** ! Tu vas mettre de la viande ?

3. Oui, j'ajouterai du **bœuf** et du **poulet**. Pas de **porc** aujourd'hui.

4. Super ! Et comme entrée, on peut avoir du **pain** et du **fromage** ?

5. Bien sûr ! Et pour le dessert, j'ai fait de la **glace**.

6. Parfait ! Demain, on pourrait essayer une recette avec du **riz**.

7. Oui, bonne idée. On ira acheter du **riz** après notre promenade à la **plage**.

8. La **plage** ? J'aurais préféré la **montagne**.

9. D'accord, alors demain, montagne et **riz** !

✤ In French, to form the past participle of regular -er verbs, replace the -er ending with -é, as in "manger" becoming "mangé" to mean "eaten."

DAY 61: FOOD AND NUTRITION II 🌱

1. Today, I'm going to make **pasta** with **butter** and **pepper**.
2. Oh, I really like **pasta**! Are you going to add any meat?
3. Yes, I'll add some **beef** and **chicken**. No **pork** today.
4. Great! And for the starter, can we have some **bread** and **cheese**?
5. Of course! And for dessert, I've made some **ice cream**.
6. Perfect! Tomorrow, we could try a recipe with **rice**.
7. Yes, good idea. We'll go buy some **rice** after our walk on the **beach**.
8. The **beach**? I would have preferred the **mountains**.
9. Alright, then tomorrow, mountains and **rice** it is!

❖ In 19th century France, the term "restaurant" originally referred to a restorative broth served to people to "restore" their health.

1. **Hier**, c'était **dimanche**, non ?

2. Oui, exactement. Et **aujourd'hui**, nous sommes **lundi**.

3. Demain sera **mardi**. J'aime bien la **semaine** parce que je vois mes amis à l'école.

4. Moi aussi. Et j'attends avec impatience le **week-end** pour me reposer.

5. **Samedi**, je vais souvent au parc près de la **rivière**. Il y a beaucoup d'**arbres** et de **fleurs**.

6. C'est beau ! **Dimanche**, je préfère rester à la maison, lire dans mon **lit** ou cuisiner.

7. Qu'est-ce que tu cuisines ?

8. Des **pâtes** au **beurre** et au **poivre**, avec du **poulet** ou du **bœuf**.

9. Ça sonne bien. J'espère que tu n'auras pas besoin d'aller à l'**hôpital** ou de voir un **médecin**.

✤ In French, when talking about activities done on specific days of the week, we use the preposition "le" before the day and the verb in its infinitive form, not the gerund.

DAY 62: DAYS OF THE WEEK 🌱

1. **Yesterday** was **Sunday**, right?
2. Yes, exactly. And **today**, we are **Monday**.
3. Tomorrow will be **Tuesday**. I really like the **week** because I see my friends at school.
4. Me too. And I look forward to the **weekend** to rest.
5. On **Saturday**, I often go to the park near the **river**. There are lots of **trees** and **flowers**.
6. That's beautiful! On **Sunday**, I prefer to stay at home, read in my **bed** or cook.
7. What do you cook?
8. **Pasta** with **butter** and **pepper**, with **chicken** or **beef**.
9. Sounds good. I hope you won't need to go to the **hospital** or see a **doctor**.

✤ In France, some people consider Tuesday the 13th unlucky, a twist from the common Friday the 13th superstition, due to the influence of Mars, the god of war, associated with Tuesday in astrology.

1. **Aujourd'hui**, il fait beau. C'est l'**après-midi** et le soleil brille.
2. Oui, mais **demain**, il va pleuvoir toute la **journée**.
3. Vraiment? Et la **nuit**, comment sera-t-elle?
4. La **nuit** sera froide. Nous sommes en **automne**, après tout.
5. J'espère que l'**hiver** ne sera pas trop long cette année.
6. Moi aussi. J'attends le **printemps** avec impatience.
7. Et l'**été**, tu aimes?
8. Oui, j'adore! Les **jours** sont longs et chauds.
9. Moi, je préfère le **matin** en **été**, quand il fait frais.

✤ To talk about liking or disliking weather in French, use "aimer" or "détester" followed by the infinitive form of weather verbs, like "aimer nager en été" (to like swimming in summer).

1. **Today**, the weather is nice. It's the **afternoon** and the sun is shining.
2. Yes, but **tomorrow**, it's going to rain all **day**.
3. Really? And the **night**, how will it be?
4. The **night** will be cold. We are in **autumn**, after all.
5. I hope that **winter** won't be too long this year.
6. Me too. I'm eagerly waiting for **spring**.
7. And **summer**, do you like it?
8. Yes, I love it! The **days** are long and warm.
9. I prefer the **morning** in **summer**, when it's cool.

✤ In France, the song "Les Feuilles Mortes" poignantly captures the melancholy of autumn, becoming an iconic reflection of the season's fleeting beauty.

1. Ma **tante** et mon **oncle** viennent mercredi.
2. Ah bon? Et ton **neveu** et ta **nièce**?
3. Oui, et aussi mon **petit-fils** et ma **petite-fille**.
4. Tu as une grande famille! Et ton **cousin**?
5. Il vient avec sa **fiancée**.
6. Super! Et ton **partenaire** de travail?
7. Mon **collègue**? Non, il ne vient pas.

✤ In French, many family-related words change their root when they become feminine, like "frère" (brother) becomes "sœur" (sister).

1. My **aunt** and my **uncle** are coming on Wednesday.
2. Oh really? And your **nephew** and your **niece**?
3. Yes, and also my **grandson** and my **granddaughter**.
4. You have a big family! And your **cousin**?
5. He's coming with his **fiancée**.
6. Great! And your **work partner**?
7. My **colleague**? No, he's not coming.

✤ In France, it's common for families to pass down recipes through generations, often considered a treasured family tale.

1. Excusez-moi, pour aller à l'aéroport, je dois **tourner** à **gauche ou à droite** ?

2. À **droite**, puis continuez **tout droit**. L'aéroport n'est pas **loin**.

3. Merci. Et pour la gare, c'est **proche** d'ici ?

4. Oui, très **proche**. **Tournez** à **gauche et c'est entre la banque et le supermarché**.

5. Parfait. Est-ce que le bus pour l'aéroport passe souvent ?

6. Oui, tous les jours, du **lundi** au **vendredi**. Il s'**arrête** juste en **bas** de cette rue.

7. Super, merci beaucoup pour votre aide.

8. De rien. Bon voyage !

✤ To give directions in French, conjugate the verb "aller" (to go) according to who is going, like "tu vas" for "you go."

1. Excuse me, to get to the airport, should I **turn left or right**?
2. **Right**, then continue **straight ahead**. The airport is not **far**.
3. Thank you. And the train station, is it **close** by?
4. Yes, very **close. Turn left and it's between the bank and the supermarket**.
5. Perfect. Does the bus to the airport come often?
6. Yes, every day, from **Monday** to **Friday**. It **stops** right **down** this street.
7. Great, thank you so much for your help.
8. You're welcome. Have a good trip!

✦ Victor Hugo wrote "Les Misérables" while in exile, journeying across Europe.

1. Je suis **excité** pour les **soldes** d'**été au centre commercial**.
2. Moi, je suis un peu **nerveux**. Et si on ne trouve pas de bonnes **réductions** ?
3. Ne sois pas **inquiet**. On va **tourner** à droite ici et arriver directement.
4. Ah, je me sens déjà plus **détendu**. J'espère être **fier** de mes achats.
5. Parfois, je suis **en colère** quand il y a trop de monde. Ça me rend **stressé**.
6. Moi, je suis juste **heureux** d'être dehors, loin de mon **appartement**.
7. Je comprends. Je suis souvent **confus** dans les grands magasins, ça me rend **anxieux**.
8. Pas de souci. Aujourd'hui, on va rester **détendus** et profiter des **réductions**.

✤ To express emotions in the past, use "être" or "avoir" in the compound tense with the appropriate past participle.

DAY 66: EMOTIONS II

1. I'm **excited** for the **summer sales** at the **mall**.
2. I'm a bit **nervous**. What if we don't find any good **discounts**?
3. Don't be **worried**. We're going to turn right here and arrive directly.
4. Ah, I already feel more **relaxed**. I hope to be **proud** of my purchases.
5. Sometimes, I get **angry** when it's too crowded. It makes me **stressed**.
6. I'm just **happy** to be outside, away from my **apartment**.
7. I understand. I often get **confused** in big stores, it makes me **anxious**.
8. No worries. Today, we're going to stay **relaxed** and enjoy the **discounts**.

✤ In the Louvre, the Mona Lisa's enigmatic smile has intrigued viewers for centuries, embodying the complex interplay of emotions in art.

1. J'ai un nouveau **smartphone** et je suis très **heureux**.
2. Ah bon ? Tu utilises quelle **application** ?
3. J'aime bien les **réseaux sociaux** et lire des **blogs en ligne**.
4. Moi, je préfère envoyer des **courriels**. C'est plus simple pour moi.
5. Tu as raison. Mais, as-tu déjà essayé de naviguer sur un **site web** avec ton **navigateur** ?
6. Oui, mais parfois, sans **Wi-Fi**, c'est difficile.
7. C'est vrai. **Internet** est vraiment important de nos jours.
8. Exactement. Et toi, tu utilises ton **smartphone** pour quoi ?
9. Principalement pour rester en contact avec ma **nièce** et mon **neveu**.

✤ In French, to talk about liking to do something related to technology and media, use "aimer + infinitive," as in "J'aime regarder des vidéos."

1. I got a new **smartphone** and I'm really **happy**.
2. Oh really? Which **app** do you use?
3. I really like **social media** and reading **blogs online**.
4. Me, I prefer sending **emails**. It's simpler for me.
5. You're right. But, have you ever tried browsing a **website** with your **browser**?
6. Yes, but sometimes, without **Wi-Fi**, it's difficult.
7. That's true. **Internet** is really important these days.
8. Exactly. And you, what do you use your **smartphone** for?
9. Mainly to stay in touch with my **niece** and **nephew**.

✤ In 1631, France introduced the world's first weekly newspaper, La Gazette, marking a pivotal moment in the evolution of the press.

1. J'ai acheté un **livre** de **poésie** hier.
2. Ah bon ? Moi, je préfère la **fiction**. Tu l'as trouvé où ?
3. Au **centre commercial**, il y avait une grande **réduction** sur tous les **romans**.
4. Intéressant ! J'aime aussi la **photographie** et le **dessin**. Tu as vu des **livres** sur l'art ?
5. Oui, il y avait une section entière avec des **livres** sur la **peinture** et la **photographie**. Et toi, tu lis quoi en ce moment ?
6. Je lis un **livre** de **non-fiction** sur mon **smartphone**. J'utilise une **application** avec **Wi-Fi**.
7. C'est pratique ! Moi, je préfère le papier. Ça me détend plus que de lire sur un écran.
8. Chacun son truc. Après la **lecture**, j'aime bien chanter.
9. Moi aussi, le **chant** c'est relaxant.

❖ In French, the participle mode can be used to describe an action related to the subject, like in "Livre lu" (Book read), where "lu" is the past participle of "lire" (to read), showing the book has been read.

1. I bought a **book** of **poetry** yesterday.
2. Oh really? I prefer **fiction** myself. Where did you find it?
3. At the **shopping center**, there was a big **discount** on all **novels**.
4. Interesting! I also like **photography** and **drawing**. Did you see any **books** on art?
5. Yes, there was an entire section with **books** on **painting** and **photography**. And you, what are you reading at the moment?
6. I'm reading a **non-fiction book** on my **smartphone**. I use an **app** with **Wi-Fi**.
7. That's convenient! I prefer paper myself. It relaxes me more than reading on a screen.
8. To each their own. After **reading**, I like to sing.
9. Me too, **singing** is relaxing.

❖ The Louvre, originally a royal palace, is now the world's largest art museum and houses the Mona Lisa.

1. Je vais à l'**aéroport** demain, je suis très **excité**.
2. Tu prends un **taxi** pour y aller ?
3. Oui, et après, je prendrai un **train** à la **gare** pour aller à l'**hôtel**.
4. Tu as beaucoup de **bagages** ?
5. Juste un **sac à dos** et une **valise**. Et toi, tu pars quand ?
6. Je reste à une **auberge de jeunesse** près de l'**ambassade**. Je suis un peu **nerveux**.
7. Pourquoi ?
8. C'est mon premier voyage seul. Mais j'ai acheté un **roman** pour lire dans le **train**.
9. Super ! Tu seras **heureux** de l'avoir fait. Bon voyage !

✤ In French, to express doing something while traveling, like "visiting Paris," use the gerund form by adding "-ant" to the verb, as in "en visitant Paris."

1. I'm going to the **airport** tomorrow, I'm very **excited**.
2. Are you taking a **taxi** to get there?
3. Yes, and then I'll take a **train** at the **station** to go to the **hotel**.
4. Do you have a lot of **luggage**?
5. Just a **backpack** and a **suitcase**. And you, when are you leaving?
6. I'm staying at a **youth hostel** near the **embassy**. I'm a bit **nervous**.
7. Why?
8. It's my first trip alone. But I bought a **novel** to read on the **train**.
9. Great! You'll be **happy** you did. Have a good trip!

✤ In France, the Chartres Cathedral is renowned for its labyrinth that pilgrims walk as a form of meditation, symbolizing a journey to spiritual enlightenment.

1. Bonjour, je dois aller à l'**aéroport**. Combien de **taxis** sont disponibles ?
2. Il y a **douze taxis** en attente.
3. Parfait. J'ai **seize** valises, est-ce un problème ?
4. Non, mais nous devons choisir un taxi de grande **taille**.
5. D'accord. À l'**hôtel**, j'aurai besoin d'une bonne connexion **Internet** pour mon **smartphone**.
6. Tous nos hôtels offrent le **Wi-Fi** gratuit. Vous pourrez utiliser toutes vos **applications** et accéder aux **réseaux sociaux** sans souci.
7. Super ! Quelle est la **prévision** du **climat** pour demain ?
8. Demain, il sera **humide** avec des chances de **tonnerre**.
9. Merci pour l'information.

❖ In French, numbers 11-20 are written as single words and do not change form based on gender or number.

1. Hello, I need to go to the **airport**. How many **taxis** are available?
2. There are **twelve taxis** waiting.
3. Perfect. I have **sixteen** suitcases, is that a problem?
4. No, but we need to choose a larger **size** taxi.
5. Okay. At the **hotel**, I will need a good **Internet** connection for my **smartphone**.
6. All our hotels offer free **Wi-Fi**. You will be able to use all your **apps** and access **social networks** without any issues.
7. Great! What's the **weather forecast** for tomorrow?
8. Tomorrow, it will be **humid** with a chance of **thunder**.
9. Thank you for the information.

✤ In the Louvre, the mysterious numbers in Leonardo da Vinci's "Mona Lisa" continue to baffle experts and numerology enthusiasts alike.

CHALLENGE NO. 7

ENGAGE IN A 15-MINUTE CONVERSATION
IN FRENCH ON EVERYDAY TOPICS.

"Rome ne s'est pas faite en un jour."
"Rome wasn't built in a day."

1. J'ai **vingt et un** livres dans ma bibliothèque.
2. Vraiment ? Moi, j'en ai **vingt-deux**. J'adore la **fiction**.
3. J'ai lu **vingt-trois romans** l'année dernière.
4. Impressionnant ! Mon livre préféré est un **poème**.
5. Hier, j'ai préparé des **pâtes** avec du **beurre** et du **poivre**.
6. Moi, j'ai cuisiné du **poulet** pour **vingt-quatre** personnes.
7. **Vingt-cinq** minutes plus tard, tout était prêt.
8. La semaine dernière, il y a eu une **tempête**.
9. Oui, et **vingt-six** maisons ont été endommagées.

❖ In French, numbers 21, 31, 41, etc., use "et un" (and one), like "vingt et un" for 21, but other numbers just combine the tens and units, like "vingt-deux" for 22.

1. I have **twenty-one** books in my library.
2. Really? I have **twenty-two**. I love **fiction**.
3. I read **twenty-three novels** last year.
4. Impressive! My favorite book is a **poem**.
5. Yesterday, I made **pasta** with **butter** and **pepper**.
6. I cooked **chicken** for **twenty-four** people.
7. **Twenty-five** minutes later, everything was ready.
8. Last week, there was a **storm**.
9. Yes, and **twenty-six** houses were damaged.

✤ In France, the mathematician Évariste Galois famously solved longstanding problems in algebra the night before he died in a duel at age 20.

1. Aujourd'hui, c'est **lundi**. Regarde le **calendrier**, nous avons un **festival** ce week-end.

2. Oui, c'est une **tradition** ici. J'ai lu l'**histoire** de ce festival dans un **musée**.

3. C'est intéressant ! La **culture autochtone est vraiment riche. Tu penses que beaucoup de touristes** viendront ?

4. Certainement. Ils arrivent souvent par l'**aéroport** ou la **gare**. Ils prennent un **taxi** pour aller à l'**hôtel**.

5. Nous devrions y aller **décontractés**. Quelle couleur préfères-tu pour ton t-shirt ? **Rouge, bleu, vert, jaune ou noir** ?

6. Je pense que **bleu** sera parfait. Et toi ?

7. **Vert** pour moi. Ça va être un bon moment pour en apprendre plus sur notre **culture**.

✤ In French, valency refers to the number of arguments a verb requires to complete its meaning, such as "manger" (to eat) needing what is eaten and "donner" (to give) needing both what is given and to whom.

1. Today is **Monday**. Look at the **calendar**, we have a **festival** this weekend.

2. Yes, it's a **tradition** here. I read the **history** of this festival in a **museum**.

3. That's interesting! The **indigenous culture** is really rich. Do you think a lot of **tourists** will come?

4. Definitely. They often arrive by **airport** or **train station**. They take a **taxi** to go to the **hotel**.

5. We should go there **casually**. What color do you prefer for your t-shirt? **Red, blue, green, yellow**, or **black**?

6. I think **blue** will be perfect. And you?

7. **Green** for me. It's going to be a good time to learn more about our **culture**.

✤ In France, there's a village called Allouville-Bellefosse that is famous for its ancient oak tree, which houses two chapels within its trunk, making it a unique place of worship.

1. Aujourd'hui, c'est le jour **quatorze** du festival.
   Veux-tu cuisiner quelque chose de spécial ?

2. Oui, je pense utiliser le **four** pour faire une tarte.
   Peux-tu me passer la **casserole** ?

3. Bien sûr. As-tu besoin de la **cuillère** ou du **couteau**
   aussi ?

4. J'ai besoin du **couteau** pour couper les fruits et de
   la **fourchette** pour mélanger les œufs.

5. D'accord. Et après, tu vas mettre la tarte dans le
   four ?

6. Exactement. Pendant ce temps, peux-tu ranger les
   assiettes et les couverts ? L'**assiette** pour la tarte est
   déjà sur la table.

7. Pas de problème. Utiliserons-nous le **grille-pain**
   demain matin ?

8. Oui, et vérifie si nous avons assez de pain dans le
   réfrigérateur ou le **congélateur**.

9. Très bien. Ce festival de cuisine est vraiment une
   belle **tradition**.

✤ In French, verbs related to cooking can be transitive (like "couper le pain" - to cut the
bread) or intransitive (like "mijoter" - to simmer), depending on whether they directly act on
an object or not.

DAY 73: COOKING AND KITCHEN II

1. Today is day **fourteen** of the festival. Do you want to cook something special?
2. Yes, I'm thinking of using the **oven** to make a pie. Can you pass me the **saucepan**?
3. Of course. Do you need the **spoon** or the **knife** as well?
4. I need the **knife** to cut the fruits and the **fork** to mix the eggs.
5. Alright. And after, you're going to put the pie in the **oven**?
6. Exactly. Meanwhile, can you put away the plates and cutlery? The **plate** for the pie is already on the table.
7. No problem. Will we be using the **toaster** tomorrow morning?
8. Yes, and check if we have enough bread in the **refrigerator** or the **freezer**.
9. Very well. This cooking festival is really a beautiful **tradition**.

✤ Julia Child, an American, brought French cuisine into American homes through her influential TV show, "The French Chef."

1. J'ai une **fièvre** et une **toux** terrible.
2. Tu as aussi des **maux de tête** ou une **allergie** ?
3. Oui, et un **mal de dent**. Je pense avoir besoin d'une **pilule**.
4. Il te faut une **ordonnance**. Va à la **pharmacie** ou à la **clinique**.
5. Ils donnent un **liquide** pour la toux ?
6. Oui, et des pilules pour la fièvre et les allergies.

✤ In French, verbs related to feeling or being, like "être malade" (to be sick), don't need a direct object to make sense.

DAY 74: MEDICAL AND HEALTH II

1. I have a **fever** and a terrible **cough**.
2. Do you also have **headaches** or an **allergy**?
3. Yes, and a **toothache**. I think I need a **pill**.
4. You need a **prescription**. Go to the **pharmacy** or the **clinic**.
5. Do they give a **liquid** for the cough?
6. Yes, and pills for the fever and allergies.

✜ Louis Pasteur, a French biologist, is celebrated for his groundbreaking work on vaccinations, saving countless lives worldwide.

1. Bonjour, tu vas à l'**école** aujourd'hui ?
2. Non, je vais à l'**université**. J'ai beaucoup de **devoirs** pour ma **matière** principale.
3. Ah, quelle **matière** étudies-tu ?
4. L'**histoire**. Aujourd'hui, nous avons une **leçon** sur les traditions anciennes.
5. Intéressant ! Et comment trouves-tu les **examens** ?
6. Difficiles, mais notre **enseignant** nous prépare bien. J'utilise toujours mon **livre** et mon **stylo** pour réviser.
7. Moi, en tant qu'**étudiant**, je préfère étudier avec des amis. Ça aide beaucoup.
8. Oui, c'est vrai. Bon, je dois y aller. Mon **emploi du temps** est très chargé aujourd'hui.
9. D'accord, bonne journée à l'**université** !

✤ In French, to express doing something to oneself, like learning, we add "se" before the verb, as in "Je me forme" (I educate myself).

1. Hello, are you going to **school** today?
2. No, I'm going to **university**. I have a lot of **homework** for my main **subject**.
3. Ah, what **subject** are you studying?
4. **History**. Today, we have a **lesson** on ancient traditions.
5. Interesting! And how do you find the **exams**?
6. Difficult, but our **teacher** prepares us well. I always use my **book** and my **pen** to review.
7. As a **student**, I prefer studying with friends. It helps a lot.
8. Yes, that's true. Well, I have to go. My **schedule** is very busy today.
9. Okay, have a good day at **university**!

✤ In France, the École 42, founded by tech entrepreneur Xavier Niel, uses a peer-to-peer learning system without any teachers or traditional classes, revolutionizing tech education.

1. J'ai besoin d'argent pour le shopping. Je vais utiliser le **distributeur automatique**.
2. Tu préfères payer par **carte de crédit** ou en **espèces** ?
3. En **espèces**, c'est plus simple. Mais, le **taux de change** est-il cher ou bon marché ici ?
4. Un peu **cher**, mais acceptable. Attention au **prix** des articles avant d'acheter.
5. Oui, je cherche quelque chose de **bon marché**. Si c'est trop cher, je demanderai un **remboursement**.
6. N'oublie pas de prendre le **reçu** pour le **remboursement**. C'est important.
7. Bien sûr. Et toi, tu achètes quelque chose ?
8. Non, je regarde seulement. J'économise mes **espèces** pour un autre jour.

✤ In French, to express reciprocity when talking about shopping or exchanging money, we use "se" before the verb, like in "Ils se donnent de l'argent" (They give each other money).

1. I need money for shopping. I'm going to use the **ATM**.
2. Do you prefer to pay by **credit card** or in **cash**?
3. In **cash**, it's simpler. But, is the **exchange rate** expensive or cheap here?
4. A bit **expensive**, but acceptable. Watch the **price** of items before buying.
5. Yes, I'm looking for something **cheap**. If it's too expensive, I'll ask for a **refund**.
6. Don't forget to take the **receipt** for the **refund**. It's important.
7. Of course. And you, are you buying anything?
8. No, just looking. I'm saving my **cash** for another day.

✿ In France, the iconic comic book series "Asterix" has sold over 380 million copies world-wide, significantly boosting the country's publishing economy.

1. Bonjour, je voudrais une table au **restaurant**, s'il vous plaît.

2. Bien sûr, voici le **menu**. Quelle **entrée** désirez-vous ?

3. Je prendrai une **salade**, merci. Et comme **plat principal** ?

4. Avez-vous un **sandwich** ou un **toast** avec **confiture** ?

5. Oui, nous avons les deux. Et pour le **dessert** ?

6. Un **chocolat** serait parfait. Acceptez-vous la **carte** ou seulement les **espèces** ?

7. Nous acceptons les deux, et aussi les **remboursements** en cas de problème.

8. Parfait, merci beaucoup.

9. De rien, j'espère que tout sera à votre goût.

✤ In French, to say who is doing an action for someone else, we use the preposition "par" before the agent, as in "Le dîner est préparé par le chef."

1. Hello, I would like a table at the **restaurant**, please.
2. Of course, here is the **menu**. What **starter** would you like?
3. I'll have a **salad**, thank you. And for the **main course**?
4. Do you have a **sandwich** or **toast** with **jam**?
5. Yes, we have both. And for **dessert**?
6. A **chocolate** would be perfect. Do you accept **cards** or only **cash**?
7. We accept both, and also **refunds** in case of any issues.
8. Perfect, thank you very much.
9. You're welcome, I hope everything will be to your liking.

✤ In France, the tradition of "savoir-faire" in restoration is so revered that some artisans are designated as "Meilleurs Ouvriers de France" (Best Craftsmen of France) to honor their exceptional skills.

1. Aujourd'hui, je vais acheter un **amuse-bouche** pour la **table**.
2. Oui, et nous avons besoin d'une nouvelle **chaise** pour la **table** aussi.
3. Dans le salon, le **lit** est près de la **fenêtre**. C'est joli.
4. Et la **porte** du **réfrigérateur** est cassée. Il faut la réparer.
5. Oui, et le **four** ne marche pas bien. Peut-être acheter un nouveau ?
6. La **lampe** à côté de la **télévision** est très belle la nuit.
7. Oui, j'aime lire un **livre** sous cette **lampe**.
8. Moi, je préfère écouter une **chanson** à la **télévision**.
9. C'est une bonne idée. La musique rend la maison joyeuse.

✤ In French, to say you are doing something with an object, like "with a pen," you use "avec" before the object, as in "avec un stylo."

1. Today, I'm going to buy an **appetizer** for the **table**.
2. Yes, and we need a new **chair** for the **table** too.
3. In the living room, the **bed** is near the **window**. It's pretty.
4. And the **door** of the **refrigerator** is broken. It needs to be fixed.
5. Yes, and the **oven** isn't working well. Maybe buy a new one?
6. The **lamp** next to the **television** is very beautiful at night.
7. Yes, I like to read a **book** under that **lamp**.
8. I prefer to listen to a **song** on the **television**.
9. That's a good idea. Music makes the house joyful.

✦ In 17th-century France, the Hall of Mirrors in the Palace of Versailles set a new standard for opulent interior design, influencing European tastes for centuries.

1. Aujourd'hui, le **climat** est très **humide**, n'est-ce pas ?

2. Oui, et les **prévisions** météo annoncent une **tempête** avec **tonnerre** et **éclair**.

3. J'espère qu'il n'y aura pas d'**ouragan** ou de **tornade**.

4. Moi aussi. Hier, j'ai lu sur un **tremblement de terre** près d'un **volcan** actif.

5. C'est effrayant. Tu vas prendre le **train** ou le **bus** pour rentrer ?

6. Je pense prendre un **taxi** jusqu'à l'**hôtel**.

7. Bonne idée. Moi, je dois aller à l'**aéroport**. Mon **avion** part dans trois heures.

8. Sois prudent. Avec cette météo, mieux vaut partir en avance.

9. Merci, à toi aussi. Restons en contact.

❖ In French, to describe the weather using an adverbial phrase, place it after the verb, like in "Il pleut beaucoup" (It's raining a lot).

1. Today, the **weather** is very **humid**, isn't it?
2. Yes, and the weather **forecast** predicts a **storm** with **thunder** and **lightning**.
3. I hope there won't be any **hurricanes** or **tornadoes**.
4. Me too. Yesterday, I read about an **earthquake** near an active **volcano**.
5. That's scary. Are you going to take the **train** or the **bus** home?
6. I'm thinking of taking a **taxi** to the **hotel**.
7. Good idea. I have to go to the **airport**. My **plane** leaves in three hours.
8. Be careful. With this weather, it's better to leave early.
9. Thanks, you too. Let's keep in touch.

❖ In France, it's believed that stepping in a puddle can bring bad luck, especially if the sun is shining.

1. Tu veux faire une **randonnée** ce week-end ?
2. Non, je préfère aller au **cinéma** ou voir une **pièce de théâtre**.
3. Moi, j'aime la **natation**. Et toi, tu fais du **ski** ou du **snowboard** ?
4. J'adore la **danse** et la **musique**. Surtout, j'aime chanter des **chansons**.
5. Après, on pourrait aller au restaurant. Quel est le **menu** ?
6. Une **entrée**, un **plat principal** et un **dessert**.
7. Demain, il y aura une **tempête**. Les **prévisions** du **climat** ne sont pas bonnes.
8. Alors, allons au **centre commercial**. Il y a une **réduction** dans mon magasin préféré.
9. Super, j'ai besoin d'aller à l'**épicerie** aussi.

✤ In French, to talk about hobbies at a specific time, use "à" for clock times (à huit heures) and "en" for months or seasons (en juillet, en été).

1. Do you want to go **hiking** this weekend?
2. No, I'd rather go to the **movies** or see a **play**.
3. I like **swimming**. What about you, do you do **skiing** or **snowboarding**?
4. I love **dancing** and **music**. Especially, I like singing **songs**.
5. Afterwards, we could go to a restaurant. What's on the **menu**?
6. An **appetizer**, a **main course**, and a **dessert**.
7. Tomorrow, there's going to be a **storm**. The **weather forecast** is not looking good.
8. Then, let's go to the **shopping mall**. There's a **discount** at my favorite store.
9. Great, I need to go to the **grocery store** too.

✤ Victor Hugo, the celebrated French author, found solace and inspiration in his hobby of drawing, creating thousands of sketches.

CHALLENGE NO. 8

SPEAK ONLY IN FRENCH FOR AN HOUR.

"Les langues sont les clés de nombreuses portes."

"Languages are the keys to many doors."

1. Aujourd'hui, je vais au **cinéma** en **bus**. Et toi ?
2. Moi, je préfère prendre mon **vélo** pour aller à la **randonnée**.
3. Hier, j'ai vu un **film** sur les voyages en **bateau**. C'était fascinant !
4. Vraiment ? Moi, j'ai lu un livre sur les **trains**. C'est incroyable comment ils peuvent être rapides.
5. Oui, mais as-tu déjà voyagé en **avion** ? C'est encore plus rapide !
6. Non, mais j'aimerais bien. Par contre, je n'aime pas trop les **camions**, ils sont trop bruyants.
7. D'accord. Et le **métro**, tu l'utilises souvent ?
8. Pas vraiment, je préfère le **tramway**. C'est plus agréable.
9. Ah, je vois. Moi, j'aime bien marcher. C'est bon pour les **jambes** et la **tête**.

✢ In French, to indicate where an action related to transport occurs, place the adverbial of place after the verb, like in "Nous allons à Paris" (We are going to Paris).

1. Today, I'm going to the **movies** by **bus**. And you?
2. Me, I prefer to take my **bike** to go **hiking**.
3. Yesterday, I saw a **movie** about traveling by **boat**. It was fascinating!
4. Really? I read a book about **trains**. It's amazing how fast they can be.
5. Yes, but have you ever traveled by **plane**? It's even faster!
6. No, but I would like to. However, I don't really like **trucks**, they're too noisy.
7. Okay. And the **subway**, do you use it often?
8. Not really, I prefer the **tram**. It's more pleasant.
9. Ah, I see. I like to walk. It's good for the **legs** and the **mind**.

✤ In 1769, Nicolas-Joseph Cugnot built the first self-propelled road vehicle in France, effectively inventing the world's first automobile.

1. J'aime la **nature**. Veux-tu aller à la **montagne** ou à la **plage** ce weekend ?
2. La **plage** ! J'adore l'**océan**. Et toi ?
3. Moi, je préfère la **forêt**. C'est calme et beau.
4. On peut vérifier les **prévisions**. Si le **climat** est bon, on y va en **voiture**.
5. Bonne idée ! J'espère qu'il n'y aura pas de **tempête**.
6. Si le temps est mauvais, on peut visiter un **musée** sur l'**histoire** de la **ville**.
7. Oui, ou demander à notre **enseignant** des recommandations.
8. Parfait ! On prépare ça sur le **calendrier** ?
9. Oui, marquons-le pour samedi !

✤ In French, to express a cause, we often use "parce que" before explaining the reason something happens, like "Il pleut parce que les nuages sont gris" (It's raining because the clouds are grey).

1. I love **nature**. Do you want to go to the **mountains** or to the **beach** this weekend?
2. The **beach**! I adore the **ocean**. And you?
3. Me, I prefer the **forest**. It's calm and beautiful.
4. We can check the **forecast**. If the **weather** is good, we'll go by **car**.
5. Good idea! I hope there won't be a **storm**.
6. If the weather is bad, we can visit a **museum** on the **history** of the **city**.
7. Yes, or ask our **teacher** for recommendations.
8. Perfect! Shall we schedule it on the **calendar**?
9. Yes, let's mark it for Saturday!

✤ France's first national park, the Vanoise National Park, was established in 1963 to protect the Alpine ibex from extinction.

1. **Hier,** j'ai fait une randonnée en **forêt**.
2. **Aujourd'hui, je vais nager dans la rivière.**
3. Et **demain** ?
4. **Demain, je pense aller au cinéma.**
5. **Maintenant,** c'est le **matin** ou l'**après-midi** ?
6. C'est l'**après-midi**. Ce **soir**, je vais préparer le dîner.
7. Qu'est-ce que tu vas cuisiner ?
8. Je vais utiliser la **poêle** pour faire des amuse-bouches. Ils seront sur la **table** à **minuit**.
9. À **minuit** ? C'est très tard pour manger !

✤ To express purpose in French, use "pour" followed by an infinitive verb, as in "Je lis pour apprendre."

1. **Yesterday**, I went hiking in the **forest**.
2. **Today, I'm going to swim in the river**.
3. And **tomorrow?**
4. **Tomorrow, I'm thinking of going to the movies**.
5. **Now**, is it **morning** or **afternoon?**
6. It's the **afternoon**. This **evening**, I'm going to prepare dinner.
7. What are you going to cook?
8. I'm going to use the **pan** to make appetizers. They will be on the **table** at **midnight**.
9. At **midnight?** That's very late to eat!

✤ In France, it's common to start the day with a fresh baguette from the local boulangerie.

1. Je me sens **seul** maintenant.
2. Pourquoi es-tu **contrarié** ?
3. J'ai une **fièvre** et des **maux de tête**. Je suis **inquiet**.
4. Tu devrais prendre une **pilule**. Ça te rendra **content**.
5. Oui, mais je suis **nerveux** à l'idée de prendre l'avion demain matin.
6. Ne t'inquiète pas. Tu seras **détendu** et **fier** de toi après.
7. J'espère. Je ne veux pas être **en colère** ou **effrayé** pendant le vol.
8. Tu seras **ravi** quand tu arriveras. L'avion est plus rapide que le train ou la voiture.
9. Merci. Je me sens un peu mieux maintenant.

✤ A relative clause in French, which starts with "qui" for subjects or "que" for objects, gives extra information about the person or thing related to the emotion.

DAY 84: EMOTIONS III 🌱

1. I feel **lonely** now.
2. Why are you **upset**?
3. I have a **fever** and **headaches**. I'm **worried**.
4. You should take a **pill**. It will make you **happy**.
5. Yes, but I'm **nervous** about taking the plane tomorrow morning.
6. Don't worry. You'll be **relaxed** and **proud** of yourself afterward.
7. I hope so. I don't want to be **angry** or **scared** during the flight.
8. You'll be **thrilled** when you arrive. The plane is faster than the train or car.
9. Thank you. I feel a bit better now.

✤ In France, the Festival of Love, "La Fête de l'Amour," is celebrated in some villages by exchanging flowers and love letters, embodying the nation's romantic spirit.

1. Regarde, le ciel est très **bleu** aujourd'hui.
2. Oui, et les montagnes sont un peu **grises**. C'est beau.
3. Tu préfères la **montagne** ou l'**océan** ?
4. J'aime l'**océan** parce qu'il est **bleu** et grand. Et toi ?
5. Moi, je préfère la **forêt**. Elle est **verte** et calme.
6. Hier, à l'**école**, l'**enseignant** a parlé des **couleurs**.
7. Ah bon ? Et qu'est-ce que tu as appris ?
8. Que le **jaune** et le **bleu** font **vert**. C'était intéressant.
9. C'est vrai. Les **couleurs** sont amusantes à apprendre.

❖ In French, when describing colors and shapes together, use "et" (and) to join the adjectives, ensuring they both agree in gender and number with the noun they describe.

DAY 85: COLORS AND SHAPES

1. Look, the sky is very **blue** today.
2. Yes, and the mountains are a bit **gray**. It's beautiful.
3. Do you prefer the **mountain** or the **ocean**?
4. I like the **ocean** because it's **blue** and vast. And you?
5. Me, I prefer the **forest**. It's **green** and peaceful.
6. Yesterday, at **school**, the **teacher** talked about **colors**.
7. Oh really? And what did you learn?
8. That **yellow** and **blue** make **green**. It was interesting.
9. That's true. **Colors** are fun to learn about.

✤ In French art, the circle often symbolizes unity and harmony, reflecting the country's values of fraternity and equality.

1. Bonjour, **ami**. Comment vas-tu aujourd'hui ?
2. Salut ! Je vais bien, et toi ? Comment va ta **famille** ?
3. Tout le monde va bien, merci. Mon **cousin** vient me rendre visite demain.
4. C'est super ! Et comment ça se passe avec ton **partenaire** ?
5. Très bien, nous avons prévu une sortie **mercredi**.
6. Ah, et ton **collègue**, celui qui est aussi ton **voisin** ?
7. Il est très occupé **maintenant**, mais il va bien. Et toi, comment ça va avec ta **femme** ?
8. Bien, bien. Nous avons fêté notre anniversaire de **mariage** hier soir.
9. C'est merveilleux ! J'espère que vous avez passé un bon moment.

✚ To show the relationship between actions, use an adverbial clause introduced by words like "quand" (when), "parce que" (because), or "si" (if).

1. Hello, **friend**. How are you today?
2. Hi! I'm doing well, how about you? How is your **family**?
3. Everyone is fine, thank you. My **cousin** is coming to visit me tomorrow.
4. That's great! And how are things with your **partner**?
5. Very well, we have planned an outing for **Wednesday**.
6. Oh, and your **colleague**, the one who is also your **neighbor**?
7. He's very busy **now**, but he's doing well. And you, how are things with your **wife**?
8. Good, good. We celebrated our **wedding** anniversary last night.
9. That's wonderful! I hope you had a great time.

✤ In France, the famous novel "Les Liaisons dangereuses" explores the complex interplay of love and friendship through seduction and betrayal.

1. Aujourd'hui, je porte ma **veste** préférée et mes nouvelles **chaussures**.
2. Oh, j'aime beaucoup ton **chapeau** et tes **lunettes de soleil**. Tu es très élégant(e) !
3. Merci ! J'ai aussi mis ma **chemise** bleue et mon **pantalon** noir. Et toi, tu portes une belle **jupe**.
4. Oui, et regarde mes **boucles d'oreilles** et mon **collier**. Je les adore !
5. Ils sont magnifiques. Tu es prêt(e) pour aller au restaurant ?
6. Absolument ! J'ai hâte de voir le **menu**. J'espère qu'il y aura une bonne **entrée**.
7. Moi aussi. Et pour le **plat principal**, tu as une préférence ?
8. Pas vraiment, mais je ne dirais pas non à un bon **dessert**.
9. Parfait, allons-y alors. Ce sera une belle soirée.

✤ In French, to compare two items of clothing, use "plus... que" for "more... than" or "moins... que" for "less... than," like "Ce pull est plus chaud que cette veste" (This sweater is warmer than this jacket).

DAY 87: CLOTHES AND ACCESSORIES ⚘

1. Today, I'm wearing my favorite **jacket** and my new **shoes**.
2. Oh, I really like your **hat** and your **sunglasses**. You look very stylish!
3. Thank you! I also put on my blue **shirt** and my black **pants**. And you, you're wearing a beautiful **skirt**.
4. Yes, and look at my **earrings** and my **necklace**. I love them!
5. They are gorgeous. Are you ready to go to the restaurant?
6. Absolutely! I can't wait to see the **menu**. I hope there will be a good **appetizer**.
7. Me too. And for the **main course**, do you have a preference?
8. Not really, but I wouldn't say no to a good **dessert**.
9. Perfect, let's go then. It will be a lovely evening.

✤ In the 18th century, French high society was so obsessed with elaborate wigs that they would often be infested with mice.

1. As-tu vu les **actualités** à la **télévision** hier soir ?
2. Non, j'étais en train de regarder une **chaîne** sur mon **ordinateur**. Pourquoi ?
3. Il y avait un reportage intéressant. J'ai changé de **chaîne** avec la **télécommande** pour le trouver.
4. Ah, je préfère lire les **actualités en ligne** sur mon **smartphone** ou utiliser les **réseaux sociaux**.
5. Moi aussi, parfois. Tu reçois des **courriels** sur les dernières nouvelles ?
6. Oui, et toi ?
7. Oui, surtout sur ma **tablette**. C'est plus pratique que la **radio** maintenant.
8. C'est vrai. Les technologies changent la façon dont nous recevons les informations.
9. Exactement, et c'est tellement facile de rester informé.

✦ In French, to express a cause or reason, we use "parce que" before the clause that explains why something happens, as in "J'utilise mon téléphone parce que je veux envoyer un message."

1. Did you see the **news** on **TV** last night?
2. No, I was watching a **channel** on my **computer**. Why?
3. There was an interesting report. I switched **channels** with the **remote control** to find it.
4. Ah, I prefer reading the **news online** on my **smartphone** or using **social media**.
5. Me too, sometimes. Do you get **emails** about the latest news?
6. Yes, and you?
7. Yes, especially on my **tablet**. It's more convenient than the **radio** now.
8. That's true. Technology is changing the way we receive information.
9. Exactly, and it's so easy to stay informed.

✤ In France, the world's first public movie screening by the Lumière brothers in 1895 marked the birth of cinema, revolutionizing global entertainment.

1. Tu veux manger de la **viande** ou des **légumes** ce soir ?
2. Je préfère des **légumes** avec des **fruits**. Et toi ?
3. Moi, je vais prendre de la **viande**. Pour boire, tu veux quoi ?
4. Un **jus** de fruit, s'il te plaît. Et toi ?
5. Je vais prendre une **bière**. On a aussi du **thé**, du **café**, et du **lait**.
6. Non, merci. Le **jus** est parfait. Tu as entendu les prévisions du **climat** ?
7. Oui, ils ont dit à la **télévision** qu'il y aura une **tempête** demain.
8. Oh non, il faut qu'on achète de l'**eau** et des provisions.
9. Bonne idée. On peut arrêter au supermarché à **droite**.

✦ If you wanted to eat a croissant, you would go to a bakery.

1. Do you want to eat **meat** or **vegetables** tonight?
2. I'd prefer some **vegetables** with **fruit**. How about you?
3. Me, I'm going to have some **meat**. What do you want to drink?
4. A **fruit juice**, please. And you?
5. I'll have a **beer**. We also have **tea, coffee, and milk**.
6. No, thanks. The **juice** is perfect. Did you hear the weather **forecast**?
7. Yes, they said on **TV** that there will be a **storm** tomorrow.
8. Oh no, we need to buy some **water** and supplies.
9. Good idea. We can stop at the supermarket on the **right**.

✤ In France, crêpes sold from street-side stands have become an iconic snack, often filled with sweet or savory ingredients, embodying the country's love for simple yet delicious food.

1. J'ai une nouvelle **maison** avec un grand **jardin**.
2. Vraiment ? Moi, j'habite dans un **appartement** avec un petit **balcon**.
3. Dans ma **maison**, il y a quatre **chambres** et deux **salles de bain**.
4. C'est grand ! Ma **cuisine** est petite, mais j'aime mon **salon**.
5. Moi aussi, j'ai un **garage** pour ma voiture. Et toi ?
6. Non, juste une **cour** pour mon vélo. Tu es **heureux** ?
7. Oui, très **heureux**. Et toi, es-tu **excité** pour la **randonnée** demain ?
8. Un peu **nerveux**, mais **excité**. J'ai mes **chaussures** et ma **veste**.
9. Parfait ! Ce sera amusant.

✦ When talking about actions that will happen as soon as another is completed, use "dès que" followed by the future tense, for example, "Je rangerai ma chambre dès que je finirai mes devoirs."

1. I have a new **house** with a big **garden**.
2. Really? I live in an **apartment** with a small **balcony**.
3. In my **house**, there are four **bedrooms** and two **bathrooms**.
4. That's big! My **kitchen** is small, but I love my **living room**.
5. Me too, I have a **garage** for my car. And you?
6. No, just a **yard** for my bike. Are you **happy**?
7. Yes, very **happy**. And you, are you **excited** for the **hike** tomorrow?
8. A bit **nervous**, but **excited**. I've got my **shoes** and my **jacket**.
9. Perfect! It will be fun.

✤ The Palace of Versailles, originally a hunting lodge, became the grand symbol of the absolute monarchy of the Ancien Régime.

CHALLENGE NO. 9

WATCH A MOVIE IN FRENCH WITHOUT ENGLISH SUBTITLES AND SUMMARIZE THE STORY.

"Chaque petit succès est un pas vers la victoire."

"Every small success is a step towards victory."

1. Bonjour, je cherche le **magasin** de vêtements dans le **centre commercial**.
2. Ah, il est au premier étage, à côté du **supermarché**.
3. Merci beaucoup. J'ai besoin d'un **chariot** ou d'un **panier** pour mes achats ?
4. Un **panier** devrait suffire. Les **chariots** sont plus pour le **supermarché**.
5. D'accord. Et à la caisse, le **caissier** ou la **caissière** peut-il m'offrir une **réduction** ?
6. Oui, surtout si les articles sont en **solde**. Vous verrez le **prix** final sur le **reçu**.
7. Parfait, j'espère trouver de bonnes affaires. Merci pour votre aide.
8. De rien. Bon shopping !

✤ In French, to express location, use "où" (where) after a place to start a spatial clause, like "Le magasin où j'achète mes livres" (The store where I buy my books).

1. Hello, I'm looking for the **clothing store** in the **shopping mall**.
2. Ah, it's on the first floor, next to the **supermarket**.
3. Thank you very much. Do I need a **cart** or a **basket** for my shopping?
4. A **basket** should suffice. The **carts** are more for the **supermarket**.
5. Okay. And at the checkout, can the **cashier** offer me a **discount**?
6. Yes, especially if the items are on **sale**. You will see the final **price** on the **receipt**.
7. Perfect, I hope to find some good deals. Thank you for your help.
8. You're welcome. Happy shopping!

✤ In 19th century France, the Bon Marché in Paris became the world's first department store, revolutionizing retail by offering a wide range of goods in one location.

1. **Bonjour, j'ai besoin d'aide. Il y a un** feu près de chez moi. C'est une **urgence**.
2. Restez **en sécurité**. Avez-vous appelé les **pompiers** ?
3. Oui, mais je suis inquiet. Y a-t-il un **danger** immédiat ?
4. **Nous envoyons une** ambulance **et des** premiers secours. Pouvez-vous aller à un lieu sûr ?
5. **Je peux aller** à l'hôpital moi-même. Dois-je ?
6. **Oui, si vous le pouvez. Et contactez un** médecin dès que possible.
7. Merci beaucoup pour votre aide.
8. C'est notre travail. Restez en sécurité.

✦ To express purpose in French, use "pour que" followed by the subjunctive.

DAY 92: EMERGENCY AND SAFETY 🌱

1. **Hello, I need help. There's a** fire **near my place. It's an** emergency.
2. **Stay** safe. **Have you called the** firefighters?
3. Yes, but I'm worried. Is there an immediate **danger**?
4. **We're sending an** ambulance **and** first responders. Can you get to a safe place?
5. **I can go to the** hospital myself. Should I?
6. **Yes, if you can. And contact a** doctor as soon as possible.
7. Thank you very much for your help.
8. It's our job. Stay safe.

✤ During WWII, the French village of Le Chambon-sur-Lignon saved around 3,500 Jews from the Holocaust.

1. J'ai mon **passeport** et mon **visa** pour le voyage de **demain**.
2. As-tu fait la **réservation** de l'**hôtel** ?
3. Oui, et j'ai aussi acheté le **billet**. Nous devons préparer nos **bagages** maintenant.
4. Je vais prendre mon **sac à dos** et ma **valise**. Penses-tu qu'on aura besoin d'un **guide** ou d'une **carte** ?
5. Peut-être juste une **carte**. Nous serons des **touristes** aventureux !
6. Parfait. Rendez-vous à l'**aéroport** demain matin alors.
7. N'oublie pas de vérifier si tu as tout dans tes **bagages**.
8. Bien sûr, je vérifierai tout ce soir. À demain !
9. À demain, prêts pour notre aventure.

❖ Even though you might be tired, you can still enjoy visiting the Eiffel Tower.

1. I have my **passport** and my **visa** for the trip **tomorrow**.
2. Did you make the **reservation** for the **hotel**?
3. Yes, and I also bought the **ticket**. We need to prepare our **luggage** now.
4. I'm going to take my **backpack** and my **suitcase**. Do you think we'll need a **guide** or a **map**?
5. Maybe just a **map**. We'll be adventurous **tourists**!
6. Perfect. See you at the **airport** tomorrow morning then.
7. Don't forget to check if you have everything in your **luggage**.
8. Of course, I'll check everything tonight. See you tomorrow!
9. See you tomorrow, ready for our adventure.

✤ The Ritz Paris, opened in 1898, became the first hotel to offer en suite bathrooms, revolutionizing luxury accommodation.

1. J'ai un **chat** et un **chien**. Et toi ?
2. Moi, j'ai un **oiseau** et un **poisson** dans ma chambre.
3. Les **oiseaux** sont-ils difficiles à prendre en soin ?
4. Non, pas vraiment. Mais je rêve d'avoir un **cheval**.
5. Un **cheval** ? C'est grand ! Moi, je préfère les petits animaux.
6. Oui, mais j'aime aussi les **vaches**, les **moutons**, les **chèvres**...
7. Ah, tu aimes les animaux de la ferme. Et les **poulets** ?
8. Oui, et même les **cochons**. Tous les animaux me rendent **ravi**.
9. Moi aussi, les animaux me rendent **ravi**.

✤ In French, to add an explanatory clause about animals or pets, use "qui" for "who" or "which" to describe them, like in "Le chien, qui est mignon, joue dehors."

1. I have a **cat** and a **dog**. And you?
2. Me, I have a **bird** and a **fish** in my room.
3. Are **birds** hard to take care of?
4. No, not really. But I dream of having a **horse**.
5. A **horse**? That's big! I prefer small animals.
6. Yes, but I also like **cows, sheep, goats**...
7. Ah, you like farm animals. And **chickens**?
8. Yes, and even **pigs**. All animals make me **happy**.
9. Me too, animals make me **happy**.

✤ In France, a rooster named Maurice became a symbol of rural life's rights after winning a legal battle over his early morning crowing.

1. Aujourd'hui, au **bureau**, j'ai une **réunion** importante avec mon **patron**.
2. Ah bon ? Et c'est à propos de ton **emploi** ?
3. Oui, exactement. Je dois préparer une **présentation** et un **rapport** avant la **date limite**.
4. Ça semble beaucoup de travail. Tu as de l'aide ?
5. Oui, un **collègue** m'aide. Mais nous avons peu de temps.
6. Quand est la **date limite** ?
7. C'est le vingt-sept. Et toi, as-tu des projets au travail ?
8. Moi, j'assiste à une **conférence** demain. Mon **employé** s'occupe des détails.
9. Bonne chance à nous deux alors !

✤ In direct speech, we use quotation marks to repeat someone's exact words, as in: Le chef dit, "Je suis le patron."

1. Today, at the **office**, I have an important **meeting** with my **boss**.
2. Oh really? And is it about your **job**?
3. Yes, exactly. I need to prepare a **presentation** and a **report** before the **deadline**.
4. That sounds like a lot of work. Do you have any help?
5. Yes, a **colleague** is helping me. But we're short on time.
6. When is the **deadline**?
7. It's on the twenty-seventh. And you, do you have any projects at work?
8. Me, I'm attending a **conference** tomorrow. My **employee** is handling the details.
9. Good luck to us both then!

✤ Marie Curie, a Polish-born French physicist, was the first woman to win a Nobel Prize and remains the only person to win in two different scientific fields.

1. Bonjour, comment vas-tu aujourd'hui ?
2. Pas très bien, ma **tête** me fait mal et j'ai mal à la **jambe** aussi.
3. Oh, as-tu vu un docteur ?
4. Oui, il m'a dit de reposer mon **pied** et de ne pas utiliser ma **main** trop.
5. C'est important de prendre soin de son **corps**. Et tes **yeux**, ça va ?
6. Mes **yeux** vont bien, mais mon **nez** est un peu bouché.
7. Tu devrais te reposer et boire beaucoup d'eau. Et n'oublie pas de manger quelque chose.
8. Oui, je vais utiliser ma **fourchette** et ma **cuillère** pour manger doucement.
9. Bon rétablissement. Prends soin de toi.

✤ In French, free indirect speech blends the character's thoughts into the narrator's voice without using quotation marks, as if sharing someone's thoughts or speech indirectly, like saying "He felt sick" instead of "He said, 'I feel sick'."

1. Hello, how are you today?
2. Not very well, my **head** hurts and my **leg** is also in pain.
3. Oh, have you seen a doctor?
4. Yes, he told me to rest my **foot** and not to use my **hand** too much.
5. It's important to take care of your **body**. And your **eyes**, are they okay?
6. My **eyes** are fine, but my **nose** is a bit blocked.
7. You should rest and drink plenty of water. And don't forget to eat something.
8. Yes, I will use my **fork** and **spoon** to eat slowly.
9. Get well soon. Take care of yourself.

✤ In France, there's a traditional sport called "La Soule," where villages compete by carrying a ball to their opponents' territory, a game dating back to the Middle Ages.

1. Aujourd'hui, en **salle de classe**, le **professeur** a donné beaucoup de **devoirs**.
2. Oui, et il y a un **examen** demain. As-tu ton **stylo** et ton **crayon** pour étudier ?
3. Bien sûr, et j'ai aussi mon **livre** et mon **cahier** dans mon **sac à dos**.
4. Moi, j'ai oublié mon **cahier** à la maison. Peux-tu m'aider avec les **devoirs** ?
5. D'accord. Mais après, nous devons réviser pour l'**examen** ensemble.
6. Merci beaucoup. Tu es un bon **élève** et un bon ami.
7. Toi aussi. Ensemble, nous réussirons cet **examen**.

✤ In French, the verb must agree in number and person with its subject.

1. Today, in **classroom**, the **teacher** gave a lot of **homework**.
2. Yes, and there's a **test** tomorrow. Do you have your **pen** and **pencil** for studying?
3. Of course, and I also have my **book** and **notebook** in my **backpack**.
4. I forgot my **notebook** at home. Can you help me with the **homework**?
5. Alright. But after, we need to review for the **test** together.
6. Thank you so much. You're a good **student** and a good friend.
7. You too. Together, we'll succeed in this **test**.

✤ René Descartes, a famous French philosopher, often wrote in bed, believing it was the best place for thought.

1. Pour la **fête**, j'ai acheté un **cadeau**.
2. Ah oui ? Quel **cadeau** ?
3. Un **livre**. Et toi, tu aimes la **musique** et la **danse** ?
4. Oui, surtout pendant un **festival**. C'est une belle **tradition**.
5. Exactement. Et après, les **vacances** !
6. Oui, j'irai à l'**université**. Et toi ?
7. Moi, je reste ici. Je dois étudier pour un **examen**.
8. Bonne chance ! Moi, je vais profiter de la **célébration**.
9. Merci ! Amuse-toi bien avec la **musique** et la **danse**.

✤ In French, the basic sentence structure follows the order of subject-verb-object, just like in English.

DAY 99: MISCELLANEOUS II

1. For the **party**, I bought a **gift**.
2. Oh yeah? What **gift**?
3. A **book**. And you, do you like **music** and **dance**?
4. Yes, especially during a **festival**. It's a beautiful **tradition**.
5. Exactly. And then, **vacation**!
6. Yes, I'll go to **university**. And you?
7. I'm staying here. I have to study for an **exam**.
8. Good luck! I'm going to enjoy the **celebration**.
9. Thanks! Have fun with the **music** and **dance**.

✤ In France, there's a town named Y, making it one of the shortest place names in the world.

JOUR 100 : FÉLICITATIONS POUR AVOIR TERMINÉ LE MANUEL ✿

1. **Ami**, félicitations pour avoir terminé le **livre** !
2. Merci ! J'ai lu chaque **page** assise sur ma **chaise** près de la **fenêtre**.
3. Pour célébrer, je t'invite à un **café**. On peut y aller en **voiture**.
4. Super idée ! J'apporterai mon **téléphone** pour écouter de la **musique**.
5. Et après, une petite fête à la **maison** ?
6. Oui, avec un **cadeau** pour toi. Une surprise !
7. J'espère que ce n'est pas un **ordinateur**, j'en ai déjà un.
8. Non, quelque chose de spécial. Tu verras.
9. J'ai hâte ! C'est une belle **célébration**.

✦ Every sentence in French must have a subject and a verb, and they must agree in number and person.

DAY 100: CONGRATULATIONS ON COMPLETING THE MANUAL ⚘

1. **Ami**, congratulations on finishing the **book**!
2. Thank you! I read every **page** sitting in my **chair** by the **window**.
3. To celebrate, I'm inviting you to a **coffee**. We can go by **car**.
4. Great idea! I'll bring my **phone** to listen to some **music**.
5. And then, a little party at the **house**?
6. Yes, with a **gift** for you. A surprise!
7. I hope it's not a **computer**, I already have one.
8. No, something special. You'll see.
9. I can't wait! It's a wonderful **celebration**.

✤ In France, achieving success is often celebrated with a toast of Champagne, a sparkling wine exclusively from the Champagne region.

CHALLENGE NO. 10

PREPARE AND GIVE AN ORAL PRESENTATION IN FRENCH ON A TOPIC YOU ARE PASSIONATE ABOUT AND RECORD YOURSELF.

"Voyager sans rencontrer l'autre, ce n'est pas voyager, *c'est se déplacer.*"
"Traveling without meeting the other is not traveling, it's moving."

CONGRATULATIONS AND
NEXT STEPS

CONGRATULATIONS

Congratulations on completing the 100 days of learning French! Your determination and perseverance have led you to succeed in this linguistic adventure.

You are now immersed in French and have acquired a solid vocabulary base, enabling you to understand and communicate in most everyday situations. This is a remarkable achievement in such a short time!

Throughout the lessons, you have developed mental mechanisms that encourage spontaneous understanding and natural conversation in French.

Be proud of yourself. You have achieved a level of autonomy that fully opens up the doors to the language and culture of French.

．　．　．

The adventure continues! To maintain and refine your skills in French:

- Practice translating texts from English to French.
- Listen to our audios on shuffle to strengthen and refresh your vocabulary.
- Immerse yourself in the language: watch movies and listen to podcasts in French.
- If you're using Flashcards, continue their daily use.
- Communicate in French, with native speakers or via AI.

Congratulations again on this achievement! And see you soon in your continuous learning journey. Au revoir!

WHAT'S NEXT?

Your success is undeniable, and to maintain your skills, continuous practice is essential.

Here are some ideas to continue progressing:

1. Review the vocabulary from this manual with our Flashcards.
2. Elevate your skills to a new level by discovering our intermediate-level manual or by exploring other NaturaLingua resources.
3. Join our online community: share, learn, and inspire others. Your journey can enlighten new learners.
4. Watch our video training and discover the secrets to mastering a language in just 100 days.
5. Fully immerse yourself in the language to reach new heights.

6. If you're ready for a new challenge, why not start a new language with our "Learn a Language in 100 Days" collection?

Learning a language is an endless adventure. Whether you deepen your knowledge of this language or embark on a new linguistic journey, the voyage never ends.

Congratulations and good luck on your continued journey!

ADDITIONAL RESOURCES

DOWNLOAD THE RESOURCES ASSOCIATED WITH THIS MANUAL AND GREATLY ENHANCE YOUR CHANCES OF SUCCESS.

Scan this QR code to access them:

☞ **https://www.natura-lingua.com/download**

• **Optimize your learning with audio:** To significantly improve your language skills, we strongly advise you to download the audio files accompanying this manual. This will enhance your listening comprehension and pronunciation.

• **Enhance your learning with flashcards:** Flashcards are excellent tools for vocabulary memorization. We highly encourage you to use them to maximize your results. Download our set of cards, specially designed for this manual.

• **Join our learning community:** If you're looking to connect with other language enthusiasts through "Natura Lingua", we invite you to join our online group. In this community, you'll have the opportunity to ask questions, find learning partners, and share your progress.

• **Explore more with other Natura Lingua manuals:** If you like this method, note that there are other similar manuals for different languages. Discover our complete collection of manuals to enrich your linguistic learning experience in a natural and progressive way.

We are here to support you in learning the target language. For optimal results, we highly recommend downloading the audio and using the flashcards. These additional resources are designed to further facilitate your journey.

Happy learning!

ABOUT THE AUTHOR

François Trésorier is a passionate polyglot and an expert in accelerated learning. He has developed unique learning methods that have helped over 31,400 people in more than 94 countries quickly achieve their learning objectives.

With more than 7 years of research, testing, and developing innovative approaches for rapid language learning, he created the Natura Lingua method. This intuitive and natural method, based on the latest findings in cognition, enables quick language results.

When he's not creating new language learning manuals or helping his community achieve language results, François is involved in humanitarian efforts in the south and east of Ukraine.

Discover how the Natura Lingua method can transform your language learning.

Visit our website www.natura-lingua.com and join our dynamic community of passionate learners.

SHARE YOUR EXPERIENCE

Help Us Revolutionize Language Learning

I hope you found this manual enriching and useful. Our goal is to democratize this innovative and natural approach to language learning, to help as many people as possible quickly and easily achieve their linguistic goals. Your support is crucial for us. If you enjoyed this manual, we would be deeply grateful if you could take a moment to leave a review on Amazon KDP. Your feedback is not only a source of encouragement for us but also helps other language learners discover this method. Thank you immensely for your contribution to our project and best wishes on your language learning journey!

BY THE SAME AUTHOR

FIND ALL OUR NATURALINGUA BOOKS ON OUR WEBSITE

SCAN ME

We regularly add new titles to our collection. Feel free to visit our website to discover the latest releases:

http://www.natura-lingua.com/

This list is not exhaustive:

- English in 100 Days
- Spanish in 100 Days
- German in 100 Days
- Italian in 100 Days
- Portuguese in 100 Days
- Dutch in 100 Days
- Arabic in 100 Days
- Russian in 100 Days
- Chinese in 100 Days
- Japanese in 100 Days
- Korean in 100 Days

ESSENTIAL GLOSSARY

INDISPENSABLE WORDS AND THEIR MEANINGS

Above - Au-dessus	Actor/Actress - Acteur/Actrice	Afternoon - Après-midi
Airplane - Avion	Airport - Aéroport	Allergy - Allergie
Alone - Seul/Seule	Alone - Seul	Ambulance - Ambulance
And - Et	And you? - Et vous ?	Angry - En colère
Animal - Animal	Anxious - Anxieux	Apartment - Appartement
App - Appli	Appetizer - Apéritif	Appetizer - Amuse-bouche
Appetizer - Entrée	Application - Application	April - Avril
Arm - Bras	Arrival - Arrivée	Assistant - Assistant
ATM - Distributeur automatique	August - Août	Aunt - Tante
Author - Auteur/Auteure	Autumn - automne	Back - Dos
Backpack - Sac à dos	Bad - Mauvais	Baked - Cuit au four
Balcony - Balcon	Band - Groupe	Bank - Banque
Banknote - Billet	Bar - Bar	Basket - Panier
Bathroom - Salle de bain	Beach - Plage	Bed - Lit
Beef - Boeuf	Beef - Bœuf	Beer - Bière
Behind - Derrière	Beside - À côté	Between - Entre
Bicycle - Vélo	Big - Grand	Bike - Vélo
Bird - Oiseau	Black - Noir	Blog - Blog

Blue - Bleu

Boarding pass - Carte d'embarquement

Boat - Bateau

Book - Livre

Boss - Patron/Patronne

Brain - Cerveau

Bread - Pain

Brother - Frère

Brown - Marron

Browser - Navigateur

Bus - Bus

Butter - Beurre

Buy - Acheter

Cake - Gâteau

Calendar - Calendrier

Calm - Calme

Camera - Appareil photo

Canyon - Canyon

Car - Voiture

Cart - Chariot

Cash - Espèces

Cashier - Caissier/Caissière

Casual - Décontracté

Cat - Chat

Cave - Grotte

Ceiling - Plafond

Celebration - Célébration

Centimeter - Centimètre

Chair - Chaise

Channel - Chaîne

Cheap - Bon marché

Checkout - Caisse

Cheese - Fromage

Chef - Chef

Chest - Poitrine

Chicken - Poulet

Children - Enfants

Chocolate - Chocolat

Chocolate : Chocolate - Chocolate : Chocolat

Cinema - Cinéma

Classroom - Salle de classe

Climate - climat

Clinic - Clinique

Clock - Horloge

Close - Proche

Clothes - Vêtements

Cloud - Nuage

Coffee - Café

Coin - Pièce

Cold - Froid

Colleague - Collègue

Computer - Ordinateur

Concert - Concert

Conference - Conférence

Confused - Confus	Content - Contenu	Continent - Continent
Cough - Toux	Courtyard - Cour	Cousin - Cousin
Cousin - Cousin/Cousine	Cousin - Cousin(e)	Cow - Vache
Credit card - Carte de crédit	Culture - Culture	Currency - Devise
Dance - Danse	Danger - Danger	Day - Jour
Deadline - Date limite	Debit card - Carte de débit	December - décembre
Delayed - Retardé	Delighted - Ravi	Dentist - Dentiste
Departure - Départ	Desert - Désert	Dessert - Dessert
Discount - Réduction	Doctor - Médecin	Doctor - Médecin
Dog - Chien	Door - Porte	Down - Bas
Download - Télécharger	Drawing - Dessin	Drink - Boisson
Drink - Boire	Drizzle - Bruine	Dry - Sec
Ear - Oreille	Earrings - Boucles d'oreilles	Earthquake - Tremblement de terre
Egg - Œuf	Eight - Huit	Eighteen - Dix-huit
Eleven - Onze	Email - Courriel	Embassy - Ambassade
Emergency - Urgence	Employee - Employé(e)	Evening - Soir
Exam - Examen	Exchange rate - Taux de change	Excited - Excité/Excitée
Excited - Excité	Excuse me - Excusez-moi	Expensive - Cher

Eye - Œil	Face - Visage	Family - Famille
Far - Loin	Fast - Rapide	Father - Père
February - Février	Festival - Festival	Fever - Fièvre
Fiancé/Fiancée - Fiancé/Fiancée	Fiction - Fiction	Fifteen - Quinze
Finger - Doigt	Fire - Feu	Fire - Feu
First aid - Premiers secours	Fish - Poisson	Fitting room - Cabine d'essayage
Five - Cinq	Floor - Étage	Flower - Fleur
Foot - Pied	Forecast - prévisions	Forecast - Prévision
Forest - Forêt	Fork - Fourchette	Forty - Quarante
Four - Quatre	Fourteen - Quatorze	Freezer - Congélateur
Friday - Vendredi	Fried - Frit	Friend - Ami(e)
Friend - Ami	Friends - Amis	Fruit - Fruit
Fruits - Fruits	Full - Plein	Garage - Garage
Garden - Jardin	Gate - Porte	Gift - Cadeau
Goat - Chèvre	Gold - Or	Good - Bon
Good afternoon - Bonne après-midi	Good evening - Bonsoir	Good night - Bonne nuit
Goodbye - Au revoir	Granddaughter - Petite-fille	Grandparents - Grands-parents
Grandson - Petit-fils	Grass - Herbe	Green - Vert

Grey - Gris	Grilled - Grillé	Grocery store - Épicerie
Guide - Guide	Hair - Cheveux	Hand - Main
Happy - Heureux/Heureuse	Happy - Heureux	Hard - Dur
Hat - Chapeau	Have a good day - Bonne journée	Head - Tête
Headache - Maux de tête	Heavy - Lourd	Height - Hauteur
Hello - Bonjour	Here - Ici	Hi - Salut
Hiking - Randonnée	History - Histoire	Holiday - Vacances
Homework - Devoirs	Horse - Cheval	Hospital - Hôpital
Hospital - Hôpital	Hot - Chaud	Hotel - Hôtel
Hour - Heure	House - Maison	How are you? - Comment allez-vous ?
How much does it cost? - Ça coûte combien ?	How much? - Combien ?	How old are you? - Quel âge avez-vous ?
How? - Comment ?	Humid - Humide	Hurricane - Ouragan
Husband - Mari	I am - Je suis	I am [age] years old - J'ai [âge] ans
I am a [profession] - Je suis [profession]	I am fine - Je vais bien	I am from [city/country] - Je viens de [ville/pays]
I am going - Je vais	I buy - J'achète	I can - Je peux
I give - Je donne	I have - J'ai	I know - Je sais
I like music and sports - J'aime la musique et le sport	I live in [city/country] - J'habite à [ville/pays]	I love you - Je t'aime
I miss you - Tu me manques	I need - J'ai besoin	I understand - Je comprends

I watch - Je regarde	I would like - Je voudrais	I'm joking - Je plaisante
Ice cream - Glace	Ice-cream : Ice Cream - Ice-cream : Glace	In - Dans
Inch - Pouce	Indigenous - Autochtone	Injury - Blessure
Inn - Auberge	Inside - À l'intérieur	Internet - Internet
Island - Île	Jacket - Veste	Jam - Confiture
January - Janvier	Jewelry - Bijoux	Job - Emploi
Joyful - Joyeux/Joyeuse	Juice - Jus	Juice : Juice - Juice : Jus
July - Juillet	June - Juin	Jungle - Jungle
Key - Clé	Kilogram - Kilogramme	Kitchen - Cuisine
Knee - Genou	Knife - Couteau	Lake - Lac
Lamp - Lampe	Laptop - Ordinateur portable	Laptop - Portable
Large - Grand	Lawyer - Avocat/Avocate	Leaf - Feuille
Left - Gauche	Leg - Jambe	Length - Longueur
Lesson - Leçon	Light - Léger	Lightning - Éclair
Liquid - Liquide	Living room - Salon	Lock - Serrure
Long - Long	Look - Regarder	Loud - Fort
Low - Bas	Luggage - Bagages	Main course - Plat principal
Man - Homme	Manager - Directeur/Directrice	Map - Carte

March - Mars	Market - Marché	May - Mai
Maybe - Peut-être	Meat - Viande	Medicine - Médicament
Meeting - Réunion	Menu - Menu	Meter - Mètre
Midnight - Minuit	Milk - Lait	Milk : Milk - Milk : Lait
Minute - Minute	Monday - Lundi	Month - Mois
Morning - Matin	Mother - Mère	Mountain - Montagne
Mouse - Souris	Mouth - Bouche	Movie - Film
Museum - Musée	Music - Musique	My name is... - Je m'appelle...
Near - Près	Neck - Cou	Necklace - Collier
Neighbor - Voisin(e)	Nephew - Neveu	Nervous - Nerveux/Nerveuse
Nervous - Nerveux	New - Nouveau	News - Actualités
Nice to meet you! - Enchanté(e) de te rencontrer !	Niece - Nièce	Night - Nuit
Nine - Neuf	Nineteen - Dix-neuf	No - Non
Non-fiction - Non-fiction	Noon - Midi	Nose - Nez
Notebook - Cahier	Novel - Roman	November - novembre
Now - Maintenant	Ocean - Océan	October - Octobre
Office - Bureau	Okay - D'accord	Old - Vieux
On the left - À gauche	On the right - À droite	One - Un

Online - En ligne	Orange - Orange	Oven - Four
Over there - Là-bas	Painting - Peinture	Pan - Poêle
Parents - Parents	Park - Parc	Partner - Partenaire
Party - Fête	Passport - Passeport	Password - Mot de passe
Pasta - Pâtes	Pastry : Pastry - Pastry : Pâtisserie	Pen - Stylo
Pencil - Crayon	Pepper - Poivre	Pharmacy - Pharmacie
Photography - Photographie	Pie : Pie - Pie : Tarte	Pig - Cochon
Pill - Pilule	Pink - Rose	Plane - Avion
Plant - Plante	Plate - Assiette	Play - Jouer
Play - Pièce de théâtre	Please - S'il vous plaît	Poetry - Poésie
Police - Police	Police - Police	Pond - Étang
Pork - Porc	Port - Port	Prescription - Ordonnance
Presentation - Présentation	President - Président/Présidente	Price - Prix
Printer - Imprimante	Proud - Fier/Fière	Proud - Fier
Radio - Radio	Railway station - Gare	Rain - pluie
Rainbow - Arc-en-ciel	Reading - Lecture	Receipt - Reçu
Red - Rouge	Refrigerator - Réfrigérateur	Refund - Remboursement
Relative - Parent	Relaxed - Détendu/Détendue	Relaxed - Détendu

Remote control - Télécommande

Report - Rapport

Reservation - Réservation

Restaurant - Restaurant

Rice - Riz

Right - Droite

River - Rivière

Roasted - Rôti

Roof - Toit

Room - Pièce

Room - Chambre

Round - Rond

Sad - Triste

Safe - Sûr

Salad - Salade

Sale - Solde

Sandwich - Sandwich

Saturday - Samedi

Saucepan - Casserole

Scared - Effrayé

Schedule - Emploi du temps

School - École

Screen - Écran

Sea - Mer

Second - Seconde

See you later - À plus tard

Sell - Vendre

September - Septembre

Seven - Sept

Seventeen - Dix-sept

Shape - Forme

Sheep - Mouton

Ship - Bateau

Shirt - Chemise

Shoes - Chaussures

Shopping centre - Centre commercial

Shopping mall - Centre commercial

Shoulder - Épaule

Singer - Chanteur/Chanteuse

Singing - Chant

Sister - Sœur

Six - Six

Sixteen - Seize

Size - Taille

Skiing - Ski

Skin - Peau

Skirt - Jupe

Slow - Lent

Small - Petit

Smartphone - Smartphone

Snowboarding - Snowboard

Snowflake - Flocon de neige

Social media - Réseaux sociaux

Soda - Soda

Soda : Soft Drink - Soda : Boisson gazeuse	Soft - Doux	Song - Chanson
Sorry - Désolé	Soup - Soupe	South - Sud
Spoon - Cuillère	Spring - printemps	Square - Carré
Stairs - Escalier	Station - Gare	Stop - Arrêter
Stop here - Arrêtez-vous ici	Store - Magasin	Storm - Tempête
Straight ahead - Tout droit	Stream - Ruisseau	Stressed - Stressé
Student - Étudiant(e)	Student - Élève	Subject - Matière
Subway - Métro	Suitcase - Valise	Summer - été
Sunday - Dimanche	Sunglasses - Lunettes de soleil	Sunshine - ensoleillement
Supermarket - Supermarché	Swimming - Natation	Table - Table
Tall - Grand	Taxi - Taxi	Tea - Thé
Teacher - Enseignant/Enseignante	Teacher - Enseignant(e)	Teacher - Professeur
Telephone - Téléphone	Television - Télévision	Ten - Dix
Terminal - Terminal	Thank you - Merci	thank you! - Merci !
That way - Par là	The day after tomorrow - Après-demain	Theater - Théâtre
There - Là	Thirteen - Treize	Thirty - Trente
Thirty-Eight - Trente-huit	Thirty-Five - Trente-cinq	Thirty-Four - Trente-quatre
Thirty-Nine - Trente-neuf	Thirty-One - Trente et un	Thirty-Seven - Trente-sept

Thirty-Six - Trente-six	Thirty-Three - Trente-trois	Thirty-Two - Trente-deux
This way - Par ici	Three - Trois	Thrilled - Ravi
Thunder - Tonnerre	Thursday - Jeudi	Ticket - Billet
Time - Temps	Toast - Toast	Toast : Toast - Toast : Toast
Toaster - Grille-pain	Today - Aujourd'hui	Tomorrow - Demain
Tooth - Dent	Toothache - Mal de dent	Tornado - Tornade
Tourist - Touriste	Tradition - Tradition	Train - Train
Tram - Tramway	Tree - Arbre	Trolley - Chariot
Trousers - Pantalon	Truck - Camion	Tuesday - Mardi
Tuesday, - Mardi,	Turn - Tourner	Turn left - Tournez à gauche
Turn right - Tournez à droite	Twelve - Douze	Twenty - Vingt
Twenty-Eight - Vingt-huit	Twenty-Five - Vingt-cinq	Twenty-Four - Vingt-quatre
Twenty-Nine - Vingt-neuf	Twenty-One - Vingt et un	Twenty-Seven - Vingt-sept
Twenty-Six - Vingt-six	Twenty-Three - Vingt-trois	Twenty-Two - Vingt-deux
Two - Deux	Uncle - Oncle	Under - Sous
University - Université	Up - Haut	Upset - Contrarié
Username - Nom d'utilisateur	Valley - Vallée	Vegetables - Légumes
Visa - Visa	Volcano - Volcan	Waiter/Waitress - Serveur/Serveuse

Wall - Mur

Warm - Chaud

Water - Eau

Water : Water - Water : Eau

Website - Site web

Wednesday - Mercredi

Week - Semaine

Weekend - Week-end

Weight - Poids

Wet - Mouillé

What day is it today? - Quel jour sommes-nous aujourd'hui ?

What do you do for a living? - Que fais-tu dans la vie ?

What do you like? - Qu'est-ce que tu aimes ?

What is your name? - Comment vous appelez-vous ?

What time is it? - Quelle heure est-il ?

What? - Quoi ?

When? - Quand ?

Where are you from? - D'où viens-tu ?

Where do you live? - Où habites-tu ?

Where? - Où ?

Which one? - Lequel ? / Laquelle ? (depending on the gender of the noun referred to)

White - Blanc

Who? - Qui ?

Why? - Pourquoi ?

Wi-Fi - Wi-Fi

Wide - Large

Width - Largeur

Wife - Épouse

Wife - Femme

Window - Fenêtre

Wine - Vin

Wine : Wine - Wine : Vin

Winter - hiver

Woman - Femme

Worried - Inquiet/Inquiète

Worried - Inquiet

Year - Année

Yellow - Jaune

Yes - Oui

Yesterday - Hier

You're welcome - De rien

Youth hostel - Auberge de jeunesse